Book One of

Adventures With The Etheric:

THE HUMAN JOURNEY

Peter Rhodes-Dimmer

HERMES-CADUCEUS BOOKS

THE HUMAN JOURNEY
A HERMES-CADUCEUS BOOK

This edition published in the UK by Hermes-Caduceus Books

Cover illustration and Design by Nicholas Smith

Hermes-Caduceus Books is an imprint of
Hermes-Caduceus Publishing
Velma Boathouse
Broom Close
Teddington
Middlesex TW11 9RL

ISBN   1 901062 00 7

Printed in the UK by Advanced Design and Marketing

About the author......

Peter Rhodes-Dimmer has been highly successful in his business career with a proven track record in diverse hi-tech fields which range from computer graphics and software to satellite television. His special strength lies in conceptualizing new opportunities in various areas and developing them to commercial reality. Most of the businesses he has been involved with in a start-up phase are still in operation today.

His naturally enquiring mind led him into areas involving spiritual and psychic phenomena and discovery, and his conscious exploration into his own 'human journey' started in the 1980s and has grown apace since then, leading him into some extraordinary areas. He has brought his own characteristic brand of energy and communication skills to this most vital and exciting area and he has built a considerable network of people with similar interests and specialist skills. He is the author of *The Layman's Guide to the New Age* and is currently planning future additions to his *Adventures with the Etheric* series.

Together with his partner Oonagh Mary Harpur, he is the co-founder of The Global Change. Foundation dedicated to help bring about and support beneficial change with regard to the current state of humanity and its environment.

He is divorced with one son, and lives in an houseboat in an idyllic position on the River Thames with his partner Oonagh, who has shared many of his explorations in the New Age area and is featured in several of the adventures in this book.

Acknowledgements

As always, production of a book involves help and support from many people. Book One of Adventures With The Etheric: THE HUMAN JOURNEY is no exception.

I would particularly like to thank the following people:

My partner Oonagh Mary Harpur for her channelling work, which stands at the core of all our adventures, and which she has always facilitated with great love and integrity.

My editor, Nasreen Cornish, who has shown great patience and graciousness in encouraging me to get this work into a cohesive form that others would understand.

My friend David Hadda, who has recorded his penetrating observations about what it means to be human, in the form of his vast collection of poetry. I have been fortunate in being able to draw on this for poems which have been used in each chapter where they have provided the contrasting style to highlight the subject matter.

Judy A. Crookes who channels the entity Jacob whose input has been included towards the end of Chapter 7. Sandy Penny for the channelling of the entity Shilam Si Ra, extracts of which are included in Chapters 1 & 13. John Frank and his Committee who are featured in several of these stories.

Finally, all those of my friends who reviewed the draft manuscript and made many valuable suggestions that contributed to the final editing, including Cathryn McNaughton, Paula Orridge, and John Frank in the UK, Wanda Richardson, Kim DuPuis, Sue Ebling and Susan Stamm in the US and Jamila Djeffali in Switzerland.

Peter Rhodes-Dimmer

Index

INTRODUCTION

Our planet is in turmoil. Arguably it has always been in turmoil, and this constant turmoil has a purpose: it is the source of many different experiences! The planet we live on has been designed to support the human journey, the growth of physical beings with souls who started out as simple tribal folk perhaps, and have evolved through many incarnations to the complex and capable humans of today. Other beings here at this time are still at a much earlier stage in their journey, so that souls of vastly different levels of maturity are all present at one time.

Every person making this journey of discovery on Earth has his or her story, and his or her experiences along the way, some of which have no logical explanation. Sometimes an individual will very forcefully impose his story on those around him. For others it is a very private matter, internalised and never shared. Some are natural story-tellers, using their experiences to inform, possibly even to teach, those around them; although most people in the West would say that storytelling is a dying art at this, the end of the 20th century. But, whether we reveal it or not, we each have that unique story, that personal paradigm through which we see the world around us – it's a part of this state of being human in which we all exist.

By the same token, we each experience life differently. Some have a life which appears to flow easily and abundantly from the time they are born onto this planet to the time they leave. Most of us, however, have a variety of trials and tribulations along the way, which either help us to grow, or act as obstacles to stop us in our paths, depending on how we handle each situation. At some level, every situation brings its lessons, and if we are able to absorb these lessons, it brings us knowledge, and even wisdom. The difficulty, perhaps, lies in the fact that we seem to have collectively programmed ourselves into a rigid set of beliefs – what is right and wrong, what is true or false – and the effect of many of these beliefs is more illusion than reality.

However, a new factor has emerged in the late 80s and through the 90s, as many people are having experiences which are quite outside their normal frame of reference. These include everything from seeing fairies to remarkable healings, ghostly visitations, and huge life changes which appear inexplicable. Something very significant appears to be on the move for many of us! Our assumptions are all starting to be challenged, and this will soon bring the illusions tumbling down.

There is one key question which we might usefully explore therefore in this context: just what are we all doing here on planet Earth – what 'game' are we all playing as we live out our lives? And the formulation of this question naturally leads us at ask: what stage of this game have we now reached?

These questions have fascinated me for some years now, and as a result I have explored many aspects of what may be possible elements of the answers over the last few years. As I have done so I have been relentlessly pushed towards one startling conclusion, which is this:

Our present state of awareness is such that we, humanity at large, simply do not know who we really are, or the powers that are available to us. Nor are we conscious of what we are individually or collectively capable of being or creating, or indeed, the true meaning of our habitation of this planet.

It seems to me that at some level of our consciousness we have all agreed, perhaps even colluded, to see our world in such a narrow way as to exclude much of what goes on around us. This may appear as a startling, perhaps even an illogical claim. Certainly, if you apply the scientific principle: 'I must prove everything and demonstrate it as tangible fact before I can accept or acknowledge it', you will not get very far in exploring the possibility of a wider reality.

Indeed, if we do apply this need for proof in our day-to-day life, then by the standard of the scientific, arguably even God does not exist, although I know that there is a minority which holds exactly this belief or rather, lack of belief. I am not talking here about the 'old man with the white beard' image of a single entity that we tend to have as children. I refer to the acknowledgement that there is something of great significance and supreme intelligence, outside our ordinary lives, which we do not understand. If you pause to number the great religions of the world, and their followers, then it quickly becomes clear that the vast majority of the inhabitants of this planet have varying degrees of belief in a greater reality. Individual belief systems may have become shrouded in dogma, fundamentalism, or wholly out of date practices: but my question is, can all those people be wrong, or is the scientific view simply too narrow an instrument for use beyond the physical and related sciences? The fact is, underlying all the many man-made systems of control through religion, there is the same greater reality, which many choose to call God, which is a fact, a fundamental article of faith for billions of people here on planet Earth.

The same religions also speak of angelic beings, and their ancient writings allude to other intelligent entities who exist in some dimension other than the one with which we are familiar. There are many ancient and strange stories in every culture, frequently dismissed today as 'mythology', which is often a euphemism for things from a distant past which we don't understand, and which make us deeply uncomfortable if we give them any degree of credence. These stories often involve beings which today are simply not a part of our experience. When interpreted at the highest level, these ancient stories seem to suggest that our pre-history may well be very different from the theories of our scientists. It is a fact that only a small part of our occupancy of Earth is contained in recorded history, and all that remains of these earlier times is that which is held in folk history – mythology to you and me – which has been passed down the ages by word of mouth so many times, that the real meaning of the words is no longer understood. The original experience existed in a frame of reference so vastly different from our own, that it has long since become unrecognisable in the telling.

I believe that the call for 'scientific evidence', demanded by many so-called 'de-bunkers' of the strange experiences happening to people today is deeply unhelpful: it is merely an outward sign, a reflection, of a great deal of fear that our society still holds about matters regarding 'the unknown', and about those phenomena which we cannot control. From time immemorial, those who are not well understood as a result of what they have learned or experienced, have become the focus for hostility and malevolence directed at them from these de-bunkers. Because of the latter, many of the more enlightened amongst earlier communities have been subjected to the iniquities of the ducking stool, inquisitions, lynchings, excommunication, and other similar practices. These are all a demonstration of how our human fears are used by those who know how to orchestrate and manipulate such fears to maintain power over others.

The situation today is no different. It is simply that the name of science is invoked by the de-bunkers in order to judge and dismiss, or misrepresent phenomena which are outside science's own remit. If you observe the dictionary definition of the term, 'science' is clearly meant to be limited to that which can be proved in the physical world, which basis for assessing the non-physical, the transient (but sometimes dramatic) other worldly experience or aspects of mythological evidence is then clearly a nonsense!

So, to enable this book to make any sense at all, I recommend that you, the reader, approach its contents from what I call 'possibility consciousness'; that is to say, please do not judge its contents merely according to the surface arguments. This material is not scientifically-based, or measurable in these terms. It is about unusual and challenging experiences, strange communications and intuitions, and what these phenomena might mean for the reality we live in. Without agreeing or disagreeing with what you read, I ask that you simply work with it *as a possibility*. My experience leads me to believe that this is an important mechanism for exploring 'the unknown', which in turn leads to a wider understanding of new and exciting possibilities and explanations for what may really be going on in our lives.

The possibility of a process referred to as 'the Ascension' is mentioned at several points in this book. This is the metamorphosis that is now beginning to affect humanity. The Ascension is described in several different ways, but one practical way of looking at it is to see it as a process whereby we can achieve a higher viewpoint about what is going on around us than the one we currently hold. In order to do this, a willingness to explore is vital!

The most important realisation for each one of us is that we should understand our lives to be part of a journey towards finding out who we really are. It matters little the route that we choose to take, since there are an endless number of routes – from the deeply religious to the highly spiritual (an important distinction), or the plainly sceptical – all of which are valid. Of course, it is always open to us to pursue routes that are deeply negative, but this only serves to lengthen our personal journey. Eventually, regardless of how many blind alleys we may investigate, all routes will arrive at the same end, which is the attainment of a fundamentally higher state of being, that higher viewpoint and understanding of 'what is'.

There is another factor which makes this attainment crucially important. It is imperative that we recognise that many, perhaps even most of us, *are nearing the end of our journey*. This makes the need for us to understand our true purpose all the more important. As soon as we start to see our lives as a journey, they will in turn start to become more purposeful, and will unfold more rapidly.

This book contains personal recollections of a number of real and extraordinary experiences, which I have attempted to explain in story form, illustrate and link together to make a cohesive whole. They are about elements of my own journey, which has become a very exciting one for me. As I have said to friends a number of times, this is the most exciting life I have had for aeons! The reasons for putting these stories in print is, in part, to reassure others so that they can have and enjoy their own discoveries, and generate their own strange experiences which will take them further along their explorations. So, I hope this book will be of some small assistance to you, my valued reader, in your personal journey!

Have a good adventure!

> **Peter Rhodes-Dimmer.**
> *April 1996*

Chapter One

The Game Of Planetary Occupation

All the knowledge that I have gained over some years of exploring the issues involved in our individual journeys, leads me to believe that the real scenario for humanity starts out as something like this:

- that we human beings are all willing volunteers in a great cosmic experiment;

- that most of us have been here on planet Earth for many, many lifetimes, each of which is a part of an unique journey in which we have been integrating vast amounts of experience;

- that part of our 'agreement' before we incarnate here is that we forget all that went before in previous incarnations;

- and that this long journey which many have come through is now moving us towards a great metamorphosis, a consolidation of all we have learned, which each of us can now start to apply in order to assist humanity become what we were always designed to be i.e. to fully express the human blueprint.

Albert Einstein once said words to the effect that the rate of increase in human knowledge in the 20th century is so great that by the end of it humanity is bound to go through a great metamorphosis: and a major part of that metamorphosis will be of the mind. That metamorphosis is now very close at hand in the shape of a vast revelation, or more correctly, many inter-linked revelations, where the net effect is that we can begin to understand who we *really* are for perhaps the first time. We are poised on the edge of a great adventure that will encompass the whole of humanity!

What does all this mean? And if there is any truth in this claim, how can we hope to understand what is going on? Who, if anyone, can tell us the truth? What can we do to move ourselves forward?

This book uses a mixture of true stories, all experiences

which I have personally been through, and other material from a range of sources, to illustrate some of my basic understandings. My hope is that this may assist us all in gaining a wider picture of what is happening as our planet goes through a process of relentless change affecting us all, in the material world and far beyond. Another question immediately arises, which is how can we explore what may be awaiting us in the immediate future?

One of the most valuable tools for exploration which I have come across is the phenomenon of channelling. This ability is a little like mediumship, and it allows an individual, or a group, to speak directly with sentient beings in other dimensions, and outside the boundaries of our planet. In doing this work, one person with the ability to go into a slightly altered state of consciousness, and with sufficient sensitivity to be able to make contact, acts as the conduit, often in both directions, between here and other realms.

At this point I must mention that safeguards are needed if you are going to become involved in channelling. We must recognise that beings and entities in other dimensions have their issues and agendas, just as we do. It is important that channelled material is treated at all times with discernment, and if you are not comfortable with what you hear from a channel, you should withdraw and not continue with it. You also need to ensure that you are dealing with an entity that has your best interests at heart! There are a series of challenges and protocols which assist with this, and provide protection to the channeller and the people working with the entity. If you wish to investigate this, I recommend that you read a book called *Opening to Channel* by Sanaya Roman and Duane Packer (published by H.J. Kramer) which is available at many book shops, and gives you sound ways of doing this work without risk.

Now, health warning over, let us get back to the topic

of channelled material. I know of many people who have developed this skill. It appears to be a global phenomenon, which has only developed to its present scale relatively recently. Let me be quite clear in what I am saying in this context, which is that there is plentiful evidence that *large numbers of human beings are now talking regularly with those beings we know of as 'Angels, Extraterrestrials, Ascended Masters and Aliens' through the techniques of channelling.*

My experience with this phenomenon illustrates that there are many, many intelligent entities who exist in other dimensions that we are simply unaware of; entities who we can learn to talk to! I believe that we all have the latent ability to do this, and can bring it to operancy with a little assistance from those who already have the skills.

There has always been highly intelligent life outside our planet, which has been deeply involved in the progress of humanity. The reason that we have not found this abundant occupation of the Cosmos is that our scientists have simply been looking in the wrong place! We are separated not by physical distance, but by frequency; but more of this later!

Ideally, channelling should be regarded as a powerful tool for exploration, and *definitely not as an infallible oracle*. These entities appear very willing to assist us in our search for a wider understanding. It is important to understand that they are not gods, and should not be deified; but they can be powerful partners in our quest for understanding. If a channelled entity specifically starts telling you how you must run your life, there is something very wrong. The highest beings, who are the ones to work with, never do this. They may suggest direction, give perspectives, provide information. In my experience, they very rarely tell you, and **never** mandate, what you must do!

Working with this technique has convinced me that our universe is peopled with millions of intelligent beings, across civilisations with a degree of diversity we cannot really imagine, even when told! Some appear to be essentially like us, in a body that we might recognise as human-like, albeit they exist at a higher frequency than the one in which we find ourselves. Some have forms so remote from what we relate to as a body that we simply cannot visualise them, while others are in pure energy form. These beings each have their issues too, since they are also conducting an existence and a personal journey: but because of their different perspective, and what appears to be a high degree of telepathy with others of their type, some can give us deep insights into our own growth and journey.

Here, then, is a first example of channelling, received late in 1995, from a being called Shilam Si Ra (the name literally expresses the balancing principle between the light and the dark), who is speaking about the human journey from the very widest perspective. I think you will find it makes fascinating reading!

"Long, long ago, at a much earlier time in earth history, souls that today are human were more energy than matter. Matter was created and dissolved at will by the extensions of God's thoughts – the souls issuing forth from the heart and mind of God, they were the embodiment of God's thoughts.

After a time, souls began spending more time in matter and God gave them more authority to shift and change matter – to experiment – so God could learn by studying the experiments in action. These souls were given free will to follow their own inclinations. They were also given the freedom to 'be fruitful and multiply'. And so, the souls began to split themselves into pieces to be able to expand their experience, but also for the sheer fun of it! They were at play!

When a creation became boring, they returned to the Source, the Oneness, until they felt like playing again: they were truly the Children of God.

As time passed, they liked their creations, and were less willing to dissolve them on returning to the Source, so they left a little bit of themselves in form; to hold the form, in case they should want to repeat an experience. These little bits became the life force, the living beings (elementals) in the minerals, the plants, the animals, humans, etherians, and other beings not as familiar to us.

God, enjoying all that had been created, came up with an experiment, a game, so to speak. Some souls were asked to follow a set of rules, to extend themselves into matter in ever-increasing densities and complexities, to learn all the lessons to be learned from each level of experience before returning to the Source. Thus began the great cycle of Karma and Reincarnation. Each of these particular souls began with the mineral experience, moved into the vegetable experience, which incorporates the mineral into it, then into the animal experience which in turn incorporates the mineral and vegetable and adds other elements of experience including love, and then into human, which incorporates all that came before and adds mind.

All souls do not follow this same pattern, because some opted for other ways, but all who chose to participate in this game began at the same place; in the mineral kingdom. It became a sort of race to see who could learn all the lessons and return home first!

That meant all souls had to learn all lessons at all levels before beginning their ascent – the return home. Some souls, after long and arduous work, came up with an innovative idea. They could learn much faster if they divided up into separate pieces which would each learn specific, and more limited lessons. Thus, the light and dark separation, negative and positive, male and female, all the opposites were created; and the Fall of Man came about. The idea was that when all the divisions of the soul had learned all they could from the various scenarios, they would come back together, reintegrate, be whole again and eventually ascend to the oneness.

Some of the souls disagreed, and took the view that progression would be faster if the souls remained intact and did not have to divide and return to oneness later. So the race began to see which way worked better.

To cut a long story short, many of the 'group' souls that divided out to learn various lessons are now coming back together for group ascension. Along the way, the 'ascended masters' are the ones who reached the goal first and, having moved beyond physical form, decided to help the others with a few tips from their journey, having found out just how difficult it was to complete the ascent.

We are working in parallel with the planet, for the earth too is a being with a soul; a consciousness which is on its own journey of enlightenment and return to the Source. The whole solar system is also a small group soul that is part of the universal group soul...the earth has been learning the lessons of receptivity, allowing, giving totally unselfishly, somewhat the lessons of the martyr. These lessons are almost over, and the lesson plan is about to change to another set of lessons. This process is not unlike our own process when our souls moved from the mineral into the animal experience, and finally into the human experience. The earth is moving into self-consciousness, awareness of self, awareness of all beings within and without, and awareness too of a greater whole – the universal consciousness.

Even as we have parts of ourselves that have been off learning other lessons for us and are now asking for *reintegration into our whole, there are energies of the planet asking for reintegration into the planet. Thus the gateways are about to be opened and held open for these extra-planetary energies to be integrated.*

This is a multi-dimensional project running right through all dimensions which have been created to date. Beings from many realities are engaged in this project. Some of the processes will evoke powerful responses from the earth because this is reality and co-creation. There is no turning back, so let us be aware of the level at which we are working NOW! For God's sake, let us give up the war scenes and move into creativity instead of combat; co-operation instead of confrontation. Old energy is no longer useful, old images, dead weight. Let us release, cleanse, centre and balance within ourselves. The Ascension is at hand!"

So just what is this 'Ascension'? In chapter 5 you will find how the phenomenon of time is linked to frequency. For this to make any sense, we first need to understand the concept of frequency in this context.

Scientists who work at the atomic level have long known that any atom consists mostly of open space. There are extremely small bodies within the atom, mostly electrons and neutrons, which appear to move at such high speed that they give the appearance of the atom being solid. In fact, this high speed vibrational movement is energy. Further investigation has shown that the elements inside the atom are also energy.

The fact is that everything around us is some form of energy; whether it is a rock on the beach or a cloud in the sky or indeed, a shaft of light shining through that cloud. The only factor that separates them in energy terms is the frequency of the energy in question. The highest frequency we can detect is the top end of the light spectrum. More solid objects exist at a lower frequency. Our eyes, ears, nose and touch sensors are all frequency sensing devices, operating at different bandwidths.

There are many frequency ranges, such as the vast array of radio waves, that are totally outside our physical senses. However, the existence of radio demonstrates that these energy forms do indeed exist; as do many others.

The range of energies that we cannot detect with our senses are vastly greater than the ones that we can! We live in a sort of 'energy window' in a universe where a great deal of what exists falls right outside our ability to experience it.

We have, for many, many generations been in what the Bible calls 'the Fall', which, in technical terms is the steady fall down through the frequencies we experience. In other words, some of the energies we cannot see or experience today, were once within our capabilities. The concept of Ascension, which today is both much discussed and often very misunderstood, is when the process of the Fall is reversed, and we are able to access a much wider range of frequencies simultaneously, thus greatly enhancing both who we are as well as our faculties and awareness, and what we see around us! It is quite possible, for instance, that fairies and other such entities exist, but at a slightly higher frequency than we now experience. If we were living at that higher frequency in the past, we would have been able to see these entities quite clearly. If this was the case, many of our stories from the past would make reference to them, which indeed, our 'mythologies' do in great profusion!

To get back to the human journey, so here we are then, apparently willing participants in some great cosmic game that involves a journey of growth and experience. It seems to be intended that the game should have a positive 'win' as a potential outcome, in the form of a metamorphosis of the human race that comes with the ascension. And to add even greater complexity, according to the Shilam Si Ra channelling and other sources, it appears that each of us may exist in more than one place, simultaneously, as part of a group soul. So, is this something we are ready to grasp? And if so, what can we learn about this game, and the journey it implies?

Ready? Then please read on.............

To rise
      and rise
    just on its own
Is not enough –
Unless you grow aware,
          do not rule out
      that life
Has always further lives
Still higher up
        above your present sphere,
      and only
In the company
         of more and more of it
      is constant rising
Really wise.

Chapter Two

The Nature Of The Human Journey

Who am I? Why am I here? These questions are two of the oldest in the world when humans get to reflecting on life. Perhaps all is not as it seems...

With my partner Oonagh, I have experienced a great many sessions of channelling; many conversations which are apparently with beings that are totally outside the dimension we exist in, and who in our experience are very intelligent entities. In one sense, it does not really concern me to try and 'prove' the source of the information that comes to us – the fact is that it contains a great deal that causes me to think hard, and to expand my perspectives. To me, this in itself, is a good enough reason to be involved.

One being in particular, who calls himself Quazar, has worked with us for several years. He says he is 'a cosmic energy being', with no incarnated form as we would understand it. Indeed, he told us that he has only once experienced life in a physical body on our planet; and this life was not in human form! He tells us that he is a gatekeeper – that is, he stands at the crossover point between the many dimensions, and has access to many, many other entities.

Very early on in our relationship with Quazar, he showed us how to protect ourselves against unwelcome energies, so that our communications would always be clean and clear from any interference. Without such protection, channelling can be open to all sorts of mischief from beings who do not necessarily have our best interests at heart, and if the technique is to have any value, efforts need to be made to keep the communications in integrity.

In addition to the protection he taught us, Quazar also offered to be present and communicate with us at the beginning of every session, and then remain on hand whenever we were working with any other entity, as a kind of 'esoteric protector'. Indeed, Quazar has done just this ever since he first offered his services, and now he often breaks in to a channelling to warn the participants if he detects that there is any unwarranted interference. In my experience, his approach to this need for proper protection appears to provide quite a sophisticated protocol for conducting and maintaining safe and secure inter-dimensional communications.

Our channelled discussions now run to some hundreds of tapes as we record nearly every session. We have only transcribed a small portion of this to date, as the entire body of channelling comes to close on three thousand, closely-typed sheets of information. Several themes have consistently arisen, such as the assumption that the human soul is indestructible, and that most of us do indeed incarnate on this planet many times as we gain our experience as humans.

When I talk about channelling there is one important point which I must mention. A great deal of Quazar's answers does not always read well in terms of 'good English'. Throughout the book, those channellings that are verbatim are organised as conversations between two or more people (just as they were recorded) *and are in italics*. Other conversations are ones for which there is no tape, and therefore I have had to rely on memory.

It is easy to be seduced by heady excitement when you first experience channelling. I would therefore stress that it is important always to keep a little healthy scepticism in place, and to be very discerning about what one hears – there is no such thing as a perfect channel. We live in a very different environment from those in other dimensions, and we have quite different ways of communicating from theirs, so there is plenty of room for misinterpretation, even if all parties are completely in integrity, and endeavouring to communicate clearly. Nevertheless, some experienced channels of high integrity are able to bring through excellent material, which can always be recognised through its main characteristics as being deeply wise, delivered in a loving and tolerant way, and frequently highly informative. Channelling can also be extremely demanding and challenging in some of the concepts that it offers. It certainly broadens one's viewpoint!

So, bearing all of this in mind, here is an example of a conversation that was recorded and transcribed, an extract from a channelling on the very subject of how channelled communication takes place:

Quazar: *When we are channelling with you in this verbal form, as well as energy form, the words, when they are typed up, are actually carrying the energy packages in the word form. And so the reader will receive more like thirty per cent of our communication, if the words are used strictly in the form in which they are – were – chosen.*

Louise: *Would there be any concern from your point of view, that your words might be mis-interpreted?*

Quazar: *That is quite possible, and that is why we recommend that they are used in their strict form, because then the energy around them will be more purely communicated.*

Louise: *Could you please explain what you mean by 'the strict form'?*

Quazar: *We mean the words that we use are not always strictly English. The words are sometimes incoherent, incomplete, inconclusive: and the choice of words is deliberate, because they carry the tonality of the energy we are communicating with the words, so when the human brain reads the words, although the words may not strictly read as English, they carry the energy form in the tonality of the words…*

In other words there are some powerful energy transactions taking place below the surface of the words! For this reason, I have generally not attempted to 'edit' Quazar's words or indeed the words of other entities who have communicated with us, but have sometimes re-expressed the questions being asked or the responses from the various people present in 'written' rather than 'spoken' English.

Quazar has described how a human soul is first created. He tells us that the great energy beings of the Cosmos have the ability to sub-divide their attention, so as to be, in our terms, in many places at once. By expanding this principle, they have given a part of their energy to become a human soul, and go on this great adventure of discovery. So when we refer to our 'Guardian Angel', our 'Guides', or our 'Higher Self', I believe this represents a reality; we are indeed connected with a higher being in another dimension. We have been largely out of touch with this being (in the conscious sense) for a long time. We are now beginning to re-connect, and for many, those connections are growing stronger: people are becoming aware of, and in some cases integrated with, their 'higher selves'!

A second assumption that arose from our discussion is that while our bodies – which Quazar often refers to as our 'body-temples' – may die, our soul is immortal! According to Quazar, death is simply a transition to another state: precisely what is acknowledged by all major religions. Indeed, it seems to me that fear of death is one of the many instruments of control that we have been subjected to over generations, and is totally unnecessary!

All in all, we have had many revelations and adventures with Quazar. Frequently, he turns our perspectives totally inside out; not always a comfortable experience. In this next story, he gives us a completely different perspective of where humanity might fit into the overall scheme of things!

A COSMIC VIEW OF HUMANITY

Our friend, Quazar, often turns the world upside down for us! One of these rather mind-blowing occasions took place when I inadvertently asked what turned out to be a rather silly question in hindsight. But I was not to know...!

"Quazar," I asked him one day in my on-going quest for knowledge. "Could you please try to explain to me the hierarchy of the higher beings in the Cosmos?"

There was a long pause. Eventually Quazar said, "We are amused that you should ask us this question..."

Feeling somewhat...terse...at this distinctly indirect response, I said "Quazar, what did you just say to me?" Perhaps I was not entirely comfortable with the thought of having been the unwitting cause of cosmic amusement.

Another long pause and then Quazar repeated patiently, "We are amused..."

"No, no!" I cut in rather impatiently. "I heard the words. It's just that I don't understand what you mean."

Another pause. "Aaaah..." Quazar then went on to say, "Please indulge me for a few moments and I will endeavour to explain...but first, I would like you to imagine smelling a beautiful rose."

Well, this was a somewhat odd request when one is seeking knowledge of higher beings, but I didn't object. I closed my eyes for a moment or two, conjured up the mental vision of a beautiful, scented, red and yellow rose, in glorious Technicolor. It felt very restful. My brief meditation over, I went back to him.

Quazar then said, "Now, imagine watching a fine sunset..." Again, I duly closed my eyes, went into my inner space, and imagined a glorious sunset of flaming colours as the sun sank over the distant sea horizon. Wonderful...I absorbed the image and returned, almost reluctantly, and Quazar continued, "And now imagine, if you will, that you are listening to the inspiration of a great choir."

Well, that one was easy for me, as a former chorister, it was a sound that I knew well and it was one which never failed to inspire me.

"And now," With these introductory words, Quazar took me through a number of similar, powerful sensory experiences, on each occasion allowing me enough time to absorb the image of the experience.

When we had finished, there was a brief pause and Quazar said, "I would like you to consider the following. None of the situations you have so readily and so easily envisaged has any meaning to me."

His words left me stunned. Speechless. This just didn't add up. Quazar must have read my energy signals for he went on to explain.

"In the dimension in which I exist," he said, "none of these experiences are available. The only reason why I can relay them to you is at second-hand, because other beings in my dimension have experienced – in what you would call the past – incarnation on your planet. I have used these examples to illustrate something to you; the physical world that you inhabit has far greater diversity of experiences available to it than any other dimension in the Cosmos; in fact, no other dimension approaches its richness of experience in this respect.

Consider if you will that the God-head, or Universal Intelligence if you prefer that term, is always exploring, always seeking to expand the boundaries of awareness by moving sentient life into ever more challenging environments. So, a considerable time ago a decision was made across the Cosmos that the physical world would be inhabited at a physical level, just as the Cosmos is already occupied at other levels by other forms of beings. A call went out for volunteers to take part in this operation and large numbers of very accomplished beings who wished to experience the physical dimension by incarnating were selected to 'give' a part of themselves for this process. It was to be a great experiment, because as well as occupying another, and new, dimension, it had been decided that these new beings would be given free will, the ability to choose at every stage.

It was a great privilege to be chosen for this, to be at the start of what might be called 'the wheel of incarnation', in your time frame, aeons ago, as the race that would eventually evolve into and become known as human beings.

Most of you are not consciously aware of this next aspect, but as part of what you are doing on Earth you each constantly feeds back to us an enormous data bank of impressions, experiences, and energies from your physical world. You are collecting information to be assessed and reviewed by beings all the way to the Godhead. For most of you this activity is not really a part of your consciousness, but is carried out by aspects of each human that function in other dimensions.

Your physical forms, the bodily temples which you inhabit, were carefully designed and engineered so that they would be viable and effective in this very dense medium in which you exist. This level of density has meant that we, your brothers and sisters from other dimensions, could not stay in contact with you in the intimate way we do at higher frequencies. We knew that part of the plan was that you would go into The Fall. This is the process of sinking ever lower in the frequency band in which you all now live.

After much time in your dimension had passed you would be mostly out of range of much of the energy support or counselling which we could provide. It was therefore also necessary to give you complete free will; something which has never been done in the same way and to the same extent before.

We all knew that, as the freedom of this isolated dimension would increase with the continuing lowering of frequency, you, the Human species, would experiment with every conceivable way of doing things. This was to be a very rich experience indeed, and one from which we would all learn...

We knew there would come a time when the lowest possible frequency that could support human existence would be reached, and you would then start the return to full connection with the other dimensions. This meant that you would, in this time which is now coming upon you, rapidly evolve to become truly multi-dimensional creatures, capable of moving to the lowest density that sentient life has yet occupied, and of travelling to far higher frequencies as well, and that you would integrate much that you have learned during your incarnations. Much of this learning would be new experience for the rest of the Universe, to which you would bring first-hand knowledge.

Now, do you see why your question amuses us?"

I hesitated. Quazar had made such a monumental statement. I was beginning to get the drift of his explanation, but was not entirely sure what to make of it...

Quazar reinforced his message, "Humanity is at the leading edge of the development of the Universe. It is in a dimension which has vastly more potential for a diversity of experiences than any other, and these are available to it to be integrated by you. You have also been given free will in all that you do, and a great deal of assistance and protection at other levels.

Let me be clear: the human experiment is not yet over. You have not yet fully expressed the potential of your human design. So far, it has been a wonderful and brave experiment, and we know what great determination and resilience you have had to develop, in order to triumph. You have, individually and collectively, integrated the experiences of hundreds, in some cases, thousands of human lifetimes. We are all now poised, with bated breath, as you might say, for the final great move, the metamorphosis that will eventually result in the colonisation of the Universe at the physical level, and led by evolved human beings."

Quazar had once more turned my ideas topsy-turvy. Since early childhood, I had been taught in the church I attended to go down on my knees and pray to those who were 'higher' than me. Many of the psalms and hymns referred to us 'poor sinners', using the age-old paradigm of sin and forgiveness and other similar religious concepts. And here, a great energy being was saying that we were it, the leading edge with no one to look up to. It is our own adventure, conducted by us with total freedom, in accordance with the granting, at the very highest level, of free will. This new perspective totally reversed all the old paradigms! We were it: there was nothing more!

It seems that we were being told that we are the primary creators in the physical realms, of necessity almost out of touch with the higher frequency realms for many generations, and now, slowly, just starting to find our way back to connection with other realms, and with the

Godhead, in a new and potentially magnificent form!

Quazar's final words during that session echoed in my ears for a long time afterwards...

..."**You see, your question amuses us, because you refer to us as the 'higher beings'. From our perspective, you humans are at the leading edge of Universal Intelligence's grand design. Although your potential is not yet fully delivered, we see you at the pinnacle of the new, and potentially, you are the highest form of evolution there is, to date...**"

So this is it. We are the frontier for the development of sentient life! All those beings in other dimensions are looking to us to carry the day, to make a great leap forward.

What stands in our way? Mostly, it seems to me, it is our lack of focus on who we really are, and what we are doing. The very materialistic lifestyles we have developed have contributed to our disconnection, both from other dimensions in general, and from each other. In a Universe of such rich connections, many human beings suffer from and are held back by loneliness. Despite our growing connectivity with other realms, we still tend to think of ourselves as the only beings in the universe, with no peer group outside the planet. As is illustrated above, Quazar's message has been quite different.

One of Quazar's communications broached the subject of human loneliness with us in June 1994 with some astonishing revelations. On that occasion we were working with a group of friends, Michele, Gwen, Benedicta and Ken. Quazar completely turned the tables by proceeding *to interview us* on the subject. Here is what transpired:

Peter: *Quazar, I wonder if you have any specific information or messages for us today?*

Quazar: *I would like you to know that you are not alone. I am importantly wishing to speak with you on this subject. The loneliness that is deep in the hearts of the human condition is not to be treated lightly because it is present. Yet you are not alone. How many times will you need to hear, speak with, see (in whatever form), channel beings of my kind of entities being here for you, to realise that you are not alone.*

You are merely the manifesting three-dimensional form of many, many beings who are your family. Here on Earth you are one of many in your incarnations who are of one family, be it blood family, spiritual family, or community. I speak not only of the one-ness of mankind and planet Earth, but also of the oneness with us all, with the many millions, millions, millions (we spoke before of this) incalculable numbers of entities around you all the time. All of you have access to us whenever you choose.

Peter: *Quazar, we tend to know these things intellectually, with our left brains, and increasingly with our right brains as well: but, as you know, it is not a part of our day-to-day experience, and so it is always a stretch for us to connect with awareness of these many other beings. We are beginning to understand that each one of us is, in some way, a multi-dimensional being. Perhaps you could speak about this?*

Quazar: *Indeed, you each have many other incarnations both in this dimension, and others, of your essence, spirit, whatever you will. For example, Peter is one of six beings who walks the Earth with his same energy pattern and essence, precisely. You are not alone, either in this form, or in the other forms that you take in other dimensions. Peter also has other incarnations in fourth, fifth, sixth, seventh levels, dimensional levels if you will. Do not be concerned about these, it is rarely necessary for you to be aware of them very consciously: however, you may feel them at times when their troubles if you will, their challenges and excitements, are such that they can drain your energy momentarily.*

So, these are concerns that you may have from time to time, and remember that you are not alone. Peter, if I may, I wish to know from you, what it is that keeps this Human form so lonely? We have difficulty with what it is that disables you from knowing us as being with you at all times. You all have conversations with us, day in and day out, so what is this loneliness that you hold on to, that we sense and feel in your energy fields?

What is it that is the obstacle for you to know that you are not alone?

Peter:	*Quazar, I will try and give you appropriate feedback. It seems that every being that we have spoken to and worked with through channelling is telepathically connected with others of their kind and with others not of their kind. This appears to be an absolute assumption, a fundamental.*

The difficulty for human beings is that for all practical purposes, we have no conscious telepathy. We believe that telepathy is something which rarely happens to us, it's a very unusual thing, happening occasionally when we make a fleeting connection. We don't consciously have those clear, permanent connections that you experience with all the beings around us. The only way we can interact, or rather the principal way we interact, is through this tool called language.

But language is not like telepathy. It has form and structure, and it can lead to much mis-communication and mis-understanding. We often say other than we are thinking, which can have great power to mislead. So in order to go through life, all Human beings must be able to stand completely on their own a lot of the time. Of course, they have their support systems, but they are not intimately linked by the telepathic links that you and your colleagues experience. Does that help to explain the difficulty?

Quazar: *Since at this moment I have before me so many of you representative Human beings, I wish to learn from you all.*

Peter: *So would you like each person to speak of why it is that they are lonely?*

Quazar: *Thank you, yes. I do appreciate your explanation Peter, and I would also appreciate each individual's personal experience of loneliness and their source of loneliness. You say you have no telepathic abilities. If I may say so, this is simply not true! You not only have the abilities, but we are aware of the telepathic communication that goes on at all times between each of you and the other entities around you, both in three-dimensional forms and in other forms.*

There is this telepathy going on all the time. Perhaps it is that you do not recognize the conversations, as you call them, in your heads, and the messages that come to you telepathically. Perhaps this misinterpretation is just a result of your training, your education, so that you believe that what is in your head, as you say, is somehow your own thoughts, as you call them. Be not mistaken: much of what you hear (as you might interpret it) in your head is not your own thought, word, deed, mind...it is a telepathic communication from another entity.

Peter: Quàzar, I think we in this room accept that process is going on, but for us it is mostly not a part of our conscious experience, it does not feel that's the way it's happening. But I took your question to be a generic one about Humanity at large, rather than a specific question about the people in this room.

Quazar: We are interested in you particularly as advanced souls. You all have reached high levels of vibration now, and as you work at these levels with all your communications, and telepathically with so many entities, we are prompted to ask what is the cause of this continuing loneliness? This is my enquiry, for us, us entities, wish to be with you at all times, we wish to strengthen and have our relationships be omnipotent, total: and yet there is always this gap of your loneliness.

Peter: Humans generally have great difficulty in forming relationships with any being which we do not see standing in an incarnated form in front of us. Our reality is the physical world. We need a great deal of trust to work outside it, and I think that most human beings would *not stretch, at the moment, to be able to embrace the kind of conversation we are now having. But to go back to your initial question, for my own part, I rarely, nowadays, feel lonely. I therefore wonder at the question itself. Perhaps we can broaden the question to the others here and have their feedback?*

Michele: *It could be a question specifically for me, Quazar. I find it very difficult to accept the death of someone I have been closely attached to. Perhaps it's to do with attachment, but the loss of someone I felt warm and close with leaves me feeling lonely. I have experienced many deaths of people I felt close to. I find it very difficult to accept that they are not around in a body any more, even though, yes, I do sometimes have a telepathic link to them. I do have a telepathic link with you, as with everybody in this room, and others, yet the loneliness persists. If you can see your way to helping me with this, I shall be very grateful.*

Quazar: *What is the nature of this loneliness?*

Michele: *It's a feeling of hurt...I know that the heart closes down and...it's difficult to open up again...and really experience love.*

Quazar: *So the problem is not the loneliness here, the loneliness is created by the unwillingness to forgive.*

Michele: *To forgive? Who to forgive, Quazar?*

Quazar: *This you spoke of, this you said: with your forgiveness of the person who has left will come acceptance at all times of this person. There is a difficulty of forgiving the person for going away and leaving (which was not leaving, merely changing form).*

Peter: *Quazar, can I ask, in your dimension, do you have anything equivalent to loneliness?*

Quazar: *We do not understand this concept.*

Peter: *So really, you are exploring something here that has no meaning in your environment?*

Quazar: *It has no meaning to us. We wish to work with you all much more closely, in order to understand: and yet this loneliness, this sense of betrayal, abandonment, and thus the closing of the heart, the cutting off from others because of this, means that the energy between us is then cut, and we cannot so easily be at one with you.*

Peter: *Quazar, it appears that human beings have had their faculties enormously diminished. Whereas you are constantly in conscious connection with many other beings, we don't have those connections unless we are standing face-to-face with somebody and talking with them. Now, I'm simplifying it, but while we do have other connections, they are very much in the background. Our ordinary, day-to-day experience is that we are effectively cut off from each other. If you have no experience of this, it must be very difficult to imagine.*

Quazar: *It is difficult, and most important because it is now limiting our abilities, mutually, to be one with each other at all times.*

Peter: *Quazar, if we could solve this problem, it would truly be a breakthrough for humanity. We are cut off from each other, let alone forming close and intimate links with you and your colleagues. So, our present lack of conscious interconnection is a problem right here, in our three-dimensional, planetary environment where individuals can be deeply lonely through lack of support, and because they do not have conscious telepathic links. So if it's a problem here between us human beings, it's an even bigger problem for us when we are dealing with a being who is not even in our dimension.*

Quazar: *Indeed, this is true, and yet sometimes it is possible for you to experience many more beings through your telepathy, than it is through your three-dimensional form, because of your mores, and ways of socially interacting which are by definition, limiting.*

Ken: *Quazar, I should like to explain something. For many humans in this dimension, it is very hard to understand that there are beings in other dimensions, and that we are not alone. This is another form of our conditioning, that we have brought with us through many incarnations. I hope I have explained myself well enough?*

Quazar: *Thank you Ken, and so this image you have given me telepathically in your speaking is of the being, the entity, not able to see beyond your three-dimensional form?*

Ken: *Yes!*

Gweneth: *I have experienced the separation from my spiritual essence, my higher self, and this causes me to feel alone. I feel that there is something missing, and I feel sad about that. So, if we were at one with our own higher levels, we would also be at one with you, and the whole of the beings in the Universe?*

Quazar: *Thank you, Gwen, that assists my learning and understanding. The loneliness you speak of feels more like a creation of your minds, a separation, and as illustrated, an attachment, or not letting go. So what happens at some stage of evolution of the being, it has a moment when a part of its experience in life is taken away, removed for some reason. This leaves a little hole in the person's experience. Instead of filling this hole with more abundance, new experience, new possibilities, the being becomes attached to the memory of what was, and maintains a perfect hole for all time,· and therefore feels this sadness, loneliness as you call it.*

This explains for us, the energy holes we see in your auras, and in your energy forms. This represents those occasions in your whole conscious evolution, when as beings you have had the experience of separation and, instead of embracing the new possibilities and filling the space with new experiences, you have tried to hold on to what was.

This hole is like an energy bubble, a little vacuum in your energy field, which then becomes a sadness for what was, and what is not today. And what will be now, and what is tomorrow, can be new and different and exciting, when there are no bubbles for nostalgia, or for some remembrance with some attachment to what was. So the forgiveness we spoke of is really the divine love that surrounds the bubble, and releases it out into its own place that recognizes that there is, in fact, no separation.

There is only the separation created by attempting to hold to what was, treating it as

*something that is, and which is too painful to
remember and yet too painful to let go. It is,
one of your Human paradoxes, this pain of
being with the separation, and yet
experiencing the love that comes when you
embrace the separation (since all is one and
one is all).*

Benedicta: *Quazar, I would like your help. That is the
process I am going through now: first of all,
accepting a great deal of pain, and then
releasing it. Knowing how to do that; is that
again, forgiveness?*

Quazar: *Indeed, this is forgiveness of oneself, and of
those beings that you now miss, whatever it is
for you, the emotion – or energy in motion –
that you hold onto them in your memory. Often
it manifests as what you call negative energy,
anger, blame, sadness, etc. Yet this energy is
only love of yourself, held in a different form.
When you forgive yourself and forgive the
other entities, this negative energy becomes
the deep love that then brightens your being,
your energy, and fills all the bubble holes and
allows them to go away.*

Peter: *Quazar, was that feedback helpful from
your perspective?*

Quazar: *Indeed, we are now much more
understanding, and we wish to support each of
you at all times in processing this experience
of loneliness, and of your knowing that we are
always with you, and that you are not alone.*

I felt this was an extraordinary encounter! I was being
told that we are in the process of becoming no less than
multi-dimensional, cosmic human beings, and that we have

many latent faculties such as telepathic communication. It simply needs our attention, and some processing, for our telepathy to start to become fully conscious...

Can humanity really cope with these deeply profound concepts? Can we integrate them, and operate them, in our lives? And if as I believe, we can, could we also cope with the quite different reality that will undoubtedly follow?

POTENTIAL

Rejoice with me,
                    you far-off ones!
I have picked myself up
                    from bending low
So as not to give away
                    my being here –
            with nothing more to fear
At last I can get on with the show!

You far-off ones,
Rejoice with me
            now
                    that I have begun
To stride out into all my possibilities,
            I hope
                    my sheer potential
            will not henceforth
Make you expect,
                    demand to see
A lot of patent miracles from me!

Chapter Three

Discarnate Beings On Earth

It always seemed to me that there were many conflicting stories of people from many parts of the world having experiences that were in part, outside of our normal consciousness. These stories did not as a rule, conflict with each other. The conflict was with what is generally accepted as credible! They dealt with 'phenomena' that are not easily explained; and not at all by science.

The channelled cosmic entities that I have become familiar with seem to be, in the strictly physical sense, very far distant from us. Are some of these strange stories perhaps explained by the existence of other entities around us in much closer dimensions? How are the many earthly stories of ghosts, UFOs and the like explained by the cosmic beings we work with? Are we blindfolding ourselves to other important realities immediately adjacent to our own?

As I hear every such phenomenon and encounter being explained away by scientists with ever more complex and to me, deeply improbable reasoning, or sometimes by commentators resorting to simple journalistic, or pseudo-scientific 'rubbishing', it seems ever easier to engage with the possibility that the stories have another truth in them.

As I have mentioned in my introduction, one of the recommendations I always make when someone sets out to explore in these areas is to work in what I call 'possibility consciousness'. This means being willing to work with strange ideas as being a possibility, rather than trying to judge or justify them in the early stages, thus allowing far more information to emerge as the exploration progresses.

Naturally, I have asked Quazar and his colleagues many questions on the subject of life outside our dimension, especially 'discarnate entities' that appear as ghosts and other phenomena. Here are some of the answers...

Peter: *The phenomenon of ghosts has been experienced and reported by a lot of humans on this planet. I would like to understand and explore with you what it is that we see when a human being experiences a ghost. Could you speak about this, please?*

Quazar: *We speak of many forms, these take so many different forms. Each of you here experiences the world quite differently from each other: some of you base your view of the world on what you hear, your hearing is the most valid part of your experience; you learn from sounds that you hear and you repeat sounds from what you hear. Others are more visionary; they remember the look or the picture of any experience. Yet others work primarily with feelings that they experience.*

So if there is a ghost, a discarnate entity, it is all that you are, present here among us, but with no body. So if you are seen in the form of a ghost, you are actually present as a human being but you have no physical form. So now, how does your friend experience you?

A person who had hearing as their most advanced form of experience may hear, speaking to him, the person who has died. The person who has seeing as their most advanced form of experiencing may see your energy form just as some human beings can see the energy form around the physical bodies of other human beings, so that when the body is gone you will still see just energy, and it will be your classic image of a ghost, a white energy form. Those of you who feel, or sense, as your main input, will experience the ghost as a cold breeze, a tingling, or as a 'dusting' sensation on your body. These are different ways, and we give you a most simplistic model.

Peter: *I recently listened to someone who reported seeing a troop of Roman soldiers passing through a very old building. He saw them in great detail, not just as a white energy and not just in passing, but as perfect representations of physical bodies, present and moving through the building for some minutes — but clearly not physical. This seems to be very different from a classic ghost.*

Quazar: *Indeed. This is not a ghost in the form of a discarnate human being; this is an experience that is coming to you more and more as part of the quickening of the human species. As you spin your energy systems faster, the higher up the frequency you move between the space-time boundaries, and so it becomes like watching a video and seeing the bits in between the film.*

Peter: *So in this case what was experienced is something that happened at a higher energy frequency, and in some way, the being who is experiencing this is crossing the time and frequency boundaries – is this correct?*

Quazar: *Indeed! We will not, though, judge whether it was a higher or lower frequency, in this context; just different...*

There appear to be other forms of ghost, too. A major category is those entities, mischievous beings from other dimensions, who set out to disturb us. They can be removed by an appropriate invocation, a very simple form of exorcism.

Then there are some 'classic' ghosts who are trapped here. They cannot leave because some vital aspect of what they were doing here on Earth while in their physical body was never completed. These unfortunates can also be exorcised and allowed to move on, and in my view, it is a kind act, and a necessary action, to do just this.

Others are elementals, those beings we once experienced as fairies, who are by nature rather simple and very mischievous! They can occasionally reach our physical world, and with the 'quickening' of the energies around us, I believe this may start to happen far more often than in the recent past. Many a sceptic is destined to be shaken by this type of experience in the near future!

I have had several personal ghostly experiences, which have illustrated some of the variations very clearly to me.

In the early 1980s, I was involved in a rather dramatic ghost incident. This, it seemed to me, belonged to yet another category, neither discarnate human, nor an event from the far past brought to the present time by some time anomaly. See what you think...

GHOST ATTACK

For a considerable number of years leading up to the mid-1980s, my business was running a company which installed complex computer systems into TV stations. This was a specialised area, and for some years my head of sales was Sheelah, a highly competent lady who I had recruited from a major TV station. She was an invaluable asset to the company and I was, and remain, personally very fond of her. Until the time she decided to leave the firm in order to start a family, we formed an excellent business team. We thoroughly enjoyed the interaction (an important part of our work), with the various bosses in the rather heady environment of

broadcasting. One of our major clients was Anglia Television.

At the time of this story Anglia had very smart offices in Park Lane, London. The building had a view across this busy thoroughfare; a rather monstrous, eight-lane 'drag' constantly filled with fast-moving London traffic, which forms a stark and surrealistic contrast to the green tranquillity of Hyde Park. The park lies on the opposite side of Park Lane, and stretches out serenely into the distance, covering an area of several square miles right in the heart of the busy metropolis.

This particular incident occurred on a day when Sheelah and I had an afternoon business appointment at Anglia. On this occasion I parked my car near the Serpentine, an artificial lake in the middle of Hyde Park. Sheelah and I walked the pleasant half-mile or so through the park to Anglia's offices to deliver a sales presentation. In the event, both the presentation and the business discussion which then followed overran considerably, and by the time we left Anglia it was getting dark.

In order to return to the car, Sheelah and I took the subway under Park Lane, emerging at the access point into the Park. We then proceeded to walk the half-mile or so along the unlit park road. We had reached a little more than half-way, when without warning something quite weird began to happen. First of all, I suddenly had the strangest feeling...I should explain that I am highly sensitive to my environment and I definitely had the sensation that the atmosphere enveloping us had changed remarkably and turned quite oppressive. This was downright eerie. I didn't much like what I was experiencing, and turned my head to look at Sheelah to see if she was getting any of this.

I could just about see her face in the gathering gloom. To my intense astonishment and alarm, I saw that Sheelah looked as if she was rooted to the ground. She gave every impression of being completely frozen – I don't mean she was merely stationary for just a moment – it was as if she had been turned to solid rock! It occurred to me that she appeared to have momentarily stepped outside of time. She seemed to be looking just past me, across my left shoulder...

Following her line of vision I turned slowly, a bit reluctantly, and there in front of me was a scene which appeared to have materialised straight out of the film *Ghostbusters*. A huge, white, whirling energy at least ten to twelve feet tall "stood" directly facing me. This energy quite definitely had a persona, and it certainly did not come across as a friendly one, although there were no actual discernible features within this entity. All I could see was a tall, whirling, amorphous mass, perhaps some three feet in width, but it felt as if one could detect a face in it though it was not apparent to the naked eye.

I was terrified! ...No, on reflection that's not quite accurate: I think I was debating whether or not to become terrified. My first reaction on seeing something so bizarre and totally outside my experience to date, was complete shock and surprise; I simply hadn't had the time to get around to terror yet!

Yes, I was certainly very taken aback, and could easily have gone into an extremely frightened state, but rather inexplicably, that was not what happened. A little to my surprise, I quickly became indignant! What was this apparition about to be challenging ME in this way? I objected rather strongly to this unwarranted intrusion and, as my objection became more clearly defined, perhaps reaching all the way into my unconscious, a most extraordinary thing happened, quite unlike anything I had heard of before.

A white band of energy suddenly launched itself from my forehead. My conscious self looked on amazed as this 'band' stretched out towards the whirling entity, forming a kind of hand at the end of it. It really looked as if I had grown an ethereal third arm. The band grew and grew outward and upward until this etheric hand was directly over the entity. It then descended slowly and inexorably, squashing the white mass beneath it, totally absorbing it like a sponge until it was eventually 'hoovered' away and disappeared completely!

I can't tell how long this process took: it may have been moments or minutes! As you might understand, I was very shaken and, when it was all over, it took me a few moments (and a few deep breaths) to regain my composure, though I was mostly in a 'this can't be happening to me' state. I turned to Sheelah and saw, to my relief, that she had come out of her temporarily frozen state and now looked rather dazed, blinking as if she had just emerged from a very deep sleep. She had absolutely no recollection, indeed no knowledge, of the incident whatsoever...

At the time, I thought that what I had experienced was probably some malevolent entity, challenging me for some reason which I had failed to understand. However, looking back on the incident, and the various areas of knowledge which I have since explored, I suspect it might have been my own higher self – the being that originally gave part of its energy to become the soul that is now me – and that I was simply not ready for this experience. This would explain how I had suppressed it so easily. My very robust response to what, in essence is another part of me, must have been a great surprise to this 'ghostly' entity!

My next ghost encounter was totally different; quite a classic, one might say! It was a haunting that occurred over some weeks, and involved someone with 'unfinished business'. Yet, for a considerable part of the time, I did not realise quite what was happening!

THE *VELMA* GHOST

Since 1983 I have lived in a houseboat called *Velma*, with stunning water views, on the river Thames at Teddington, a small town just to the west of London, England. In the first few months I was there it was the scene of a very strange haunting...

When I first saw the boat, and the garden and Victorian boathouse that goes with it, the whole property was in very poor repair, and the garden was totally unkempt. All in all, the prospect seemed quite daunting and I thought about the entire purchase long and hard. True, I really wanted a place by the river...I was recently divorced, my young son Alex was with his mother so that I only got to see him at weekends, and perhaps understandably, I was not the happiest of people at that time. At that low point in my life my first love, of the water, was calling to me and it was difficult to resist this 'siren song'. My parental home had been close to the sea on the south coast, and I greatly missed being by the water, along which I had grown up. Having always known and been involved with the sea, when I first moved to London it left a void; no great expanse of water to play on!

This was the one thing in my current state of existence which I might be able to fix. The river Thames was the best substitute for the sea which I could find, if I were to continue to work in London.

Perhaps its cool energies would assist in the healing process which I undoubtedly needed.

But this? A ramshackle houseboat with a falling down boathouse and a grossly overgrown garden? On the face of it, the proposition was a complete liability!

Before committing myself irrevocably to buying, I visited the property a number of times, and on these occasions a gracious, elderly lady called Jean, showed me around and patiently answered all my questions. She was the executor of a will which included this property as part of the estate. The owner, who had been called Madge, had died on the boat six months earlier, after an illness which had left her bedridden. Whenever I was at the property I could easily envisage that the whole site might one day be very beautiful, but there was clearly a lot of hard work involved before this stage was reached. If, indeed, it ever was!

On my third visit to the property, Jean showed me round yet again, and in her usual gracious manner painstakingly answered yet more questions. At one point she slid open the drawer of a small sideboard, to look briefly at some postcards inside. As she did so, I noticed tears in her eyes, and I realised that she was really quite upset. I apologised, assuming I might have inadvertently said something highly inappropriate, which had caused this emotional reaction.

"No, no," she said, "It's not that at all..." and explained that until Madge's death, she had also lived at *Velma*. We sat down, and her story unfolded. Originally, long before the second World War, Jean had been Madge's paid personal companion and secretary.

Madge had been a relatively wealthy woman, the owner of a substantial printing works inherited from her father. The boat, which was moved to its present site just before the War, had been a very lively place and the scene for a great deal of entertaining. Both ladies had developed connections with the glamorous world of the Theatre, and later with the new business of television, so that well-known entertainers were often party visitors. Amongst the regulars was the famous author and playwright Noel Coward, who was a native of Teddington (the local town) and tended to draw other social luminaries to his circle of cronies.

It was clear that Madge and Jean had, over a long time, become much closer and developed a very intimate relationship. As this dawned on me I realised just how painful the job of executor must be for Jean. I said something to that effect, using my best diplomatic manner! "No," said Jean, "It's not you, and it's not your fault. Frankly, the problem I find most difficult is having to deal with the house clearance people!"

I gathered that she had contacted several house clearance agents, as well as furniture and antiques dealers, to obtain quotes for clearing the place, and they were now behaving like vultures picking over the contents of what had been her summer home. I could see that this in-fighting would be most distressing for a sensitive and gentle person like her. By now, I had pretty much decided to go ahead and buy the property, despite the obvious drawbacks. A thought struck me, and as I was distinctly short of furniture, I, perhaps rather impulsively, decided to follow my intuition and said, "How would it be if I were to buy *Velma* including all the contents? If you tell me the best offer you have had, I would be happy to add say, ten per cent, and we can roll it all into one package."

She seemed greatly relieved by this, and so this is precisely what we did! I bought the entire contents of the property including a few good antiques, several household effects, and, it must be said, a great deal of rubbish that was going to take a dismayingly long time to sort through. Having struck the deal, things proceeded quickly and I moved in a few weeks later.

I quickly identified that the boathouse was the biggest mess. It is a beautiful old Victorian building, with a workshop at river level, and facilities to draw a river launch out of the water for the winter. Over the top of this workshop there is a big room approaching 800 square feet. The building has carved sandstone panels in its timber framed outer walls, stained glass windows, and a timber-lined interior which creates the feel of a small chapel within. Today, this beautiful and gracious room functions as my office, but at that time it was full, to perhaps a height of two to three feet, with accumulated rubbish and bric-a-brac. Over the years it had been used as the basement that the houseboat itself could never have – for obvious reasons! The houseboat was in a somewhat better state, but also had a great deal of clutter, which would have to be sorted, and much of it disposed of.

The trouble was, I could not just throw it all out! In amongst what was probably a ton of near-rubbish were a small number of quite valuable items, and I wanted to know just what I had bought! There was no way I could get out of it and I resigned myself to the business of going through the contents item by item. A long haul was in prospect!

I moved in, very happy with my rather shambolic lot and, with the help of my then girlfriend Karen, and clear-up weekend visits from my parents, I started the long process of bit-by-bit clearance.

At this time, my son Alex, who was then about seven years old, started to visit me and to sleep over, every second weekend. He got involved in the general clearing-out and it certainly made a good adventure for us both and helped draw us closer together! This was also when we found the letters...!

I had started to clear the bedroom in which Madge had died. Under her bed, I found a stationery box. I opened it, and inside I found two items: a notebook, and a bundle of letters held together by a blue ribbon. As I leafed through the notebook, I realised that it contained the drafts of a series of love letters. The first few were in halting French – she had obviously not got much further in her school studies than I had – and the later ones in English. My first, instinctive reaction was of distinct embarrassment!

I gathered that in their younger days, it had been the habit of the two ladies to travel to the Mediterranean coast every winter, thus avoiding the worst of the English winter. These letters were dated from immediately before the war. It appeared that on one of these winter sojourns Madge had secretly met, and fallen in love with, a young French military officer. He must have been based for some time in Geneva, to which location the letters were addressed.

The bundle of letters were all the originals. Obviously at the end of the affair, he had done what was then considered the honourable and gentlemanly thing: he had returned all her letters to her.

It was clear was that in the weeks when she was ill and dying, Madge had undoubtedly read and re-read her old love letters, perhaps many times, reliving past events and emotions. They must have been a great source of both pleasure and pain. The burning question was, what to do with them now? In the light of her probable lesbian relationship with Jean over many years, it just did not seem appropriate to hand over the letters to the executor. My intuition told me that Jean was not aware of them, and might well be very upset by their revelation. Madge had died without any children, and I had no knowledge of any family, so there was no obvious recipient for the collection, which was assuming something of the character of an 'emotional hand grenade'!

Continuing to feel distinctly embarrassed about the whole issue, I put the letters to one side promising myself to 'deal with them later'. As often happens with such resolutions, I promptly forgot about them! And, as is illustrated in a few of these stories, the consequences of my lapses of memory can sometimes be quite startling!

The following Friday, my son came to stay. We had a fun evening – I seem to remember we went out to see a film that we both enjoyed – slept well, and got up fairly early on Saturday morning. Soon Alex, who has a healthy appetite, was asking what was for breakfast, and I promised to cook a full English breakfast, a treat we always enjoyed together. As I was in the middle of preparing this mammoth meal, he asked "Are we going to see Karen today?" Karen was quite a favourite with Alex, but I had made no plans to see her as yet. "Couldn't we ask her to breakfast?" asked Alex. This seemed like a good idea to me, so I called her and explained what we had in mind. "Great!" exclaimed Karen. "I'm just getting into the bath, so I'll be there in about forty-five minutes." I carried on with the preparations; started the sausages cooking, cleaned the mushrooms, and scrambled the eggs just ready to pour in the pan. Everything was timed to the moment Karen would walk through the door. Soon it was close to serving time, and Karen was due any minute.

At that time the kitchen was located rather low in the boat, and the kitchen window was set in such a way that if anyone walked across the lawn outside, the person slaving away at the stove (usually me!) would only see their bottom half. So, as I worked away, I was not surprised to see the bottom half of a female figure wearing black trousers, walking across the lawn to the conservatory which serves as the land-based entrance to *Velma*. I called to Alex, "I think she's here," and we both rushed to the door to greet our lady friend. However...

...Seconds later the conservatory was in full view and...NO-ONE!

There really is nowhere to hide around *Velma's* conservatory, and the person who had just walked in had simply disappeared. We searched a little, and then I shrugged it off. Obviously, Karen was playing some kind of joke on us.

She walked through the door some five minutes later. "Were you here," I began rather cautiously, "five minutes ago?"

"Are you crazy!" came the ready response. "I was just getting into the bath when I took your call and it's been a real rush to get here." I explained what had happened. For a few moments we were all puzzled, not to mention confused, but then the inviting smells of breakfast diverted our attention to the pressing issue of the moment – FOOD! We said no more and tucked into a large breakfast.

I thought no further of the incident until a few days later. That morning I was once again in the boat, looking across the lawn towards the boathouse, which had by then been partly cleared and pressed into use as my office, when I saw what I was sure was the same woman as I had seen on the previous Saturday. Once again she wore black trousers, but now I could see all of her, and that she was wearing a white blouse. She walked up the steps to the office, and went inside.

"I'll get to the bottom of this!" I thought, and hurried to intercept the intruder. I crossed the lawn purposefully, ran up the steps to the boathouse, grasped the door handle and found...that it was securely locked! This was the first trip I had made to the office that day, and I had not yet unlocked it. The keys to the boathouse were still in the houseboat.

As I realised that there was simply no way anybody could have gained entrance to the office, I felt a sudden cold chill...and the hairs on the back of my neck stood on end! "Just what is going on?" I demanded of no-one in particular!

Over the next few days, the woman 'intruder' was seen several times; not just by me, but by visitors as well as neighbours. I was strangely relieved by this. At least it proved that I was not going *totally* insane. But my mysterious, uninvited visitor remained elusive. Perhaps I was simply not paying enough attention to her visitations, because in a few days, she was to raise 'the game' to a new level!

It happened two weeks later. There was a regatta at the local Sailing Club, which is just round a bend in the river from the houseboat, perhaps five hundred yards away. It was a fine, clear and sunny day, with a stiff breeze blowing: ideal, if somewhat challenging racing weather for the large, over-canvassed sailboats my friends and I all sailed in. We raced our yachts all day, after which the participants gathered at the bar to relax over a few pints. After an hour or so of slaking our thirsts, someone said, "Well, what's on this evening?" After checking all round, the answer seemed to be a resounding "Nothing!"

So, by way of a magnanimous gesture, I said, "Let's make a party at *Velma*..."

...and that's just what we did. People brought food, drink, music, and within the hour guests had arrived, and things were definitely warming up.

By ten o'clock in the evening the party had been in full swing for at least two hours. The party room, on the lower deck, was hot, noisy, and full of cigarette smoke. Music blared, people talked at their loudest in an effort to be heard, there was dancing...indeed, everyone was having a good time.

At one point there was a lull in the music, when I overheard Jack, an elderly friend who was quite prescient, saying to someone, "You know, it's strange, I have travelled all over the world, and experienced some strange things in my time, and I would say that there is some presence on this boat. I really feel something quite powerful here." Almost immediately, I was aware that two people on my other side were having a similar conversation...and THEN it happened...

The whole environment changed in a moment. The entire scene around me was now cold, clear of smoke, and silent. The people all looked like they were part of a 'freeze frame' on a video recording, absolutely stationary, as if suspended in time. I have no idea if this lasted for many minutes or a fraction of a second, but after what seemed like an interminable time, a voice in my head said, *"It's all to do with the letters..."*

I instantly remembered the bundle of love letters, left forgotten many weeks earlier, and I felt the same blush of embarrassment I had experienced when I first set eyes on them. In almost the same thought, I was also made aware of their real potential for causing pain and difficulty to others if they were ever made public. I had already acknowledged to myself that Jean, for instance, might certainly be very hurt by them. This realisation took the form of a conversation, with some unknown party, entirely conducted inside my head. As a result of this brief debate, I solemnly resolved to burn the letters at the earliest opportunity. Indeed, I made it a silent promise, and ...

...immediately, the room went straight back to normal, but many people had picked up on what had just taken place. "Did you notice a..." "I could have sworn that...." "I think I must have drunk too much...!" Everyone knew that *something* had happened, but it was, for the rest of those present, a confused and unclear experience. No-one was entirely sure as to exactly what had occurred. They were a fairly reliable group of people, for in the assembled company was the Club Commodore (a senior figure in the City of London banking world), as well as a local solicitor, not to mention a bank manager, and a local councillor, later to become the Lady Mayor; all together an upright gathering (when they were not sailing or partying!). All of those present were aware that something out of the ordinary had occurred.

It did not however constrain us from partying the rest of the evening and into the small hours!

The following morning a small group of us (the hard core that remained) made a little bonfire with dry sticks and timber, and I ceremonially delivered my promise of the evening before. One by one the letters, and the notebook were burnt, and went up in a blue haze of smoke, leaving behind a very small pile of ashes. The hauntings – for I am convinced that is what they were – ceased, and the woman in black trousers and white blouse has simply never been seen again. It's as if my action had done had removed her reason for staying around *Velma*, and allowed her to move on: business finished, no need to stay any longer!

Later, I consulted a clairvoyant friend who was quite sure that our ghost had indeed been Madge, the lady who had died on the boat. My friend thought that the now discarnate soul who was once Madge had been so worried about the potential distress that the letters might cause, that she would not leave and go to the next stage of her soul-journey until the matter had been dealt with. I, as the most likely person to assist, had been given many hints, but had not realised that something specific was expected of me until the rather more dramatic happenings at the party!

If this is the case, I hope and trust that the lady is now safely at rest! I believe she must be, since she has never been seen again. In the meantime, there was one more incident to come in relation to the *Velma* Ghost... When cleaning out the last contents of the cupboards in the boathouse, we found a photograph album, in which the two ladies who had occupied *Velma* for so long appeared in many of the pictures. It was easy to identify Madge. In every photograph, she was wearing black trousers, and a white blouse!!

Today, a fine drawing of Madge, the *Velma* Ghost, pictured as a younger woman aged perhaps thirty and resplendent in a ball gown, hangs in the houseboat. She looks powerful and every inch a great beauty. Perhaps the picture can pay some small tribute to her determination and resolve in coming back from other planes, in order to make sure that a close and intimate friend was not upset by revelations of a secret affair that was better hidden!

As I said, this was a 'classic' haunting. Whenever such a thing occurs, I feel that those of us who are still on the Earthly plane have a responsibility to assist the being in question. As often as not, they are trapped, and wish to move on, and I believe that we can, with a little guidance, sometimes assist in resolving their issues and help them to go. In the case of the *Velma* Ghost, my action had helped in resolving the problem. I was pleased to have been able to assist; even if I had been very slow off the mark!

Some hauntings are far more trivial than the *Velma* Ghost, perhaps rather easier to dismiss as tricks of the imagination. Indeed, one such, a far less spectacular but amusing haunting, occurred some years later at *Velma*. Here is the story...

THE CHRISTMAS CAT

In December of 1986, I invited two American friends, Ann and Charles, to come visit for Christmas. I had got to know them very well during my four years of living for part of the time in New York, and they were always great company. They arrived a few days before Christmas, quickly settled in, and the party began. We were all having a great time! Many friends called in, and the spirit of Christmas was building apace.

Several times over the first few days, Ann mentioned a cat she had seen around the houseboat, with which, being something of a 'cat person', she quickly formed a relationship. Apparently this particular cat was a large blue Persian.

There are often cats passing through the garden beside the houseboat. Indeed, I have long joked about the territorial rights over my property belonging to ducks, geese, swans, foxes, cats and other assorted wildlife as being somewhat greater than those of its human occupants: we appeared to be about tenth in line in the priorities! I thus responded to the cat story with mild interest but without attaching any particular importance to it, not realising that Ann thought that I owned it. Just to be clear, there is no 'ship's cat', and I had not owned any animal since long before the time of this story, but I forgot to tell Ann this. Also, at the time I could not recall ever actually seeing this particular cat, something else I probably should have mentioned, but didn't.

The cat saga continued, with Ann making quite a few passing references to this particular animal, until about the fifth day of Ann and Charles's arrival, when she and I were both in the kitchen talking away about goodness knows what. All of a sudden, she went quite pale, appeared totally thunderstruck, and sat down rather abruptly.

"Ann, what on earth is the matter?" I asked, concerned at her appearance and obvious shock.

It was some moments before she was able to speak, and then she said, in some agitation, "It's...your cat, Peter..." She was hesitating over her words.

"But Ann, I simply don't own a cat!" I said. I realised a moment later that this statement only seemed to make matters worse.

By now Ann was very distressed, so before pursuing the subject further, I took a little time to comfort her. I reverted to the old English cure-all of a cup of tea, always a safe move in a crisis! When we had tea brewed and poured, and things had settled down a little, I asked her, in her own good time, to describe to me what exactly had happened to create such a shock.

Ann told me she had encountered this cat several times during her stay at the houseboat, had talked to him and stroked him...and she and the cat had generally made a fuss of each other, as humans and cats so often do. She described him again, as a big male Persian, with a luxurious blue coat. She had met the cat both inside and outside the houseboat, so of course she naturally assumed that I owned the animal.

She hesitated over the next part of her narrative. Apparently, while we had been talking just a few moments earlier, the cat was sitting on a high kitchen stool to my right, generally minding its own business and quietly cleaning itself – entirely unnoticed by myself! Ann was quite definite about this, and of course, its behaviour had appeared quite normal to her! Then, as she watched it, the animal stood up, stretched, and casually jumped down from the stool.

The next move came as, to Ann's great shock, the cat sauntered over toward the kitchen wall...and simply passed right through it, disappearing from sight through the very fabric of the houseboat! The point she indicated was several feet from the nearest door or window, and there was nowhere that an animal could quickly disappear to; indeed, as Ann described it, she had seen the body progressively vanish *through the wall!* A solid wall, with the back half of a cat protruding from it, had clearly been more than Ann could take!

It was my turn to be shaken, and we talked about it often over the next couple of days trying to figure out what happened, but without any conclusion. However, as with many things of this nature, in a few days it faded from my attention, and I forgot all about the incident during the remaining time of the holiday...

The following summer, I happened to be looking out over the lawn from the upper floor of the houseboat, when I saw a large blue Persian cat, strolling nonchalantly across the open space. Something about the cat stirred my memory as I vaguely remembered Ann's shocking experience, and I looked hard at the animal. Then, I made the mistake of blinking momentarily and...the cat was gone! And there was nowhere close by to run to or hide, so it appeared to have simply de-materialised. I did several quick double-takes!

It was only then that I remembered all the details of Ann's story, the previous Christmas!

Ever since, I have had occasional visits from a big blue Persian, who seems perfectly real and solid to me, and I have even stroked the cat several times. So, I ask myself, is it the same cat, or is there indeed a phantom as well? Or perhaps cats simply have powers to move between dimensions that we humans don't really know about, as indeed I have often suspected!

In the light of the experiences I have re-told here, you, the reader might well assume that I believe in Ghosts! Indeed, you assume correctly! But I do not believe that they can harm us, or that we should be frightened by them. Often, it is likely that we can help them to move on. The sense I have is that the changes around us mean that, for a while, such things may become very commonplace. But, as the energies around us build up, eventually they will cause all these entities to finally be released, and allow them to move on...

Collaborators of the Light:
Don't laugh
      – or even smile –
When you
      with your inveterate,
          cosmos-sized sense of fun
Can see us running into traps
That stare you in the face,
      the eyes – I dare say –
          you don't have,
    while those
We here do have
Can't even see
      what's going on
Close to our noses,
      and even less
          behind our eyes,
    let alone past the stars!

So we are also blind
To you who
      – we are told –
Live all around,
      within us,
Everywhere!
How can you be surprised
We often panic
      and here and there
Despair!
Be fair!

Chapter Four

Origins – The Seeding And Development Of Humanity

Another good 'universal' question that many of us have philosophised about for generations is 'where did we come from?' Once, in the far distant past, we may have all been energy beings (as described by Shilam Si Ra in Chapter One), but there must have been many, many stages, and a great deal of lost history, between that time and now. I have never been convinced by Darwinian theory, that we simply developed from other anthropoids by natural selection. While there is much good sense in theories of natural selection, it seems to me to be less than the whole story! All that I have learned and experienced illustrates to me the probability that there were others involved – advanced races from outside this planet, who knew all about genetic engineering at levels far beyond our skills in this field, even today. I believe that they used those skills to help create us!

Here, then, is an experience I had in the form of a vivid, and oft-repeated dream: a dream that first opened up for me the possibility of another origin of humanity on this planet, and one that was radically different from what I had always been told...

THE SPACE CAPTAIN

During my twenties I had absolutely no idea about things happening in other dimensions, or about any of the latent human powers! But I did have a great many dreams...sometimes highly realistic dreams, which would appear to be more like living a situation in the most detailed way, rather than conventional dreaming. These dreams repeated themselves many times. It was almost as if someone was saying to me, 'You're supposed to get this, and you will only move on when you have got the message'.

The most vivid of these dreams seemed to be like

situations that I really had experienced, or were quite specific in some way. They were also highly personal to me, and while I was coming to terms with them I didn't feel comfortable about discussing them with anyone. There was no one I could consult about them anyway, so for many years I kept them to myself.

The strongest and most dramatic of these dreams, was a highly-detailed and most glorious Technicolor epic. I saw myself as the second-in-command on a great ship. But this was no ordinary ship, it was a scientific survey vessel, in orbit around planet Earth...in other words, a spaceship!

The team who worked around me were all human beings; or at least humanoid in form. We operated as a tightly-knit group, well-bonded, and with a strong sense of purpose. As the second-in-command, one of my functions was to be the communications officer: we appeared to have a lot of contact with new civilisations, and the way that we presented ourselves was crucially important. So the task of communications was a major responsibility.

My commanding officer was a big, well-rounded and kindly old man, who appeared as something of a father figure to us all. He had a huge experience of command but this had not always been totally successful: indeed he had been sent on this mission in a great hurry, and told that if he failed this time he would be permanently grounded. Having already worked with him on several occasions, I had got to know him rather well, and I felt that this was something which would have broken him after all his years on board ship. It was the only life he knew. I found myself propping him up in many ways, giving him moral support, a helping hand over tactical and strategic advice, and lending him a willing ear over many personal issues.

The particular mission which I am about to describe came right out of the blue and took us all by surprise. We had been the nearest available resource when something dramatic went wrong on planet Earth, and we were pressed into service.

The situation appeared to be as follows: human beings were newly seeded on the planet. They had been 'created' there, by a form of very advanced genetic engineering. Our ship's crew was part of a group of highly developed humanoid beings from other sectors of the galaxy who had worked for some thousands of years to develop a whole new genetic coding – primarily the DNA – for the new human being, which was to be a very specific and powerful upgrade on the current humanoid model, as it were.

The new human was to have several additional faculties, opening up many exciting possibilities, although the journey for humanity would be a long one before all these faculties were released and came to fruition.

Our group of genetic engineers had taken some of the local anthropoid stock, the humanoid in its most basic form, on the planet, and genetically engineered the radical change in these beings in two steps, each to occur one generation apart. The new humans that emerged had initially been 'guided' and cared for by the advanced humanoid beings, who had been disguised to look exactly like their charges, and whose task was to give the young humans some of the basic understanding which would allow them to start developing for themselves.

At the time of our ship's visit this seeding task had ended some generations ago, and apart from occasional monitoring visits, the new humans were left pretty much on their own, to allow this great experiment to progress without undue external interference.

However, a routine monitoring visit around earth by a small ship with few technical facilities observed something dramatic which was emphatically not part of the genetic plan. In fact, it had all the makings of an imminent catastrophe! The new human beings had begun to cross-breed with the local animal stock.

This development was totally foreign to the humanoid life-forms (of which I was one!) who were responsible for this great genetic experiment to create a new and potentially more capable, race of humans. They were never inclined to mate with animal life forms, or possibly even genetically unable to do so. However, the powerful new human genes seemed to possess this ability, and the result was a number of enormous aberrations being seen on the planet; bizarre beings which were half human and half...well, a range of other animals.

We only have to look into our mythology with its tales of strange half-human/half-beastly creatures, or observe the gargoyles decorating certain old buildings to see that they probably contain the far distant memories of this kind of incident, and illustrate the variety and craziness which resulted. Many of these creatures were tremendously deformed, in great pain, and had no understanding of how to function properly or of their purpose. A total nightmare translated into grotesque reality. It was a situation that required the greatest compassion, and all involved felt dreadful about the task we now faced, but it was clear that the whole human genetics project, that had taken centuries to plan and get started, was at risk because of this disastrous development.

We were there simply because we were the nearest, technically well-equipped ship when this dramatic news broke! We had to abort our current project, itself an important mission, and at zero notice we were sent in to clean up this mess quickly and, as far as possible, painlessly, and get the human experiment back on track. Among other things, it meant that a great, unpleasant purge had to be carried out on these unfortunate mutations who were in such physical pain. None of the crew enjoyed this task in the least, but we all understood just how much was a stake, and reluctantly got on with it. Once this tragic task was over, it would also mean that further genetic work would have to take place on the new human 'breeding stock'. This was also going to be very difficult by sheer weight of numbers alone, as there were already some thousands of humans spread out all over the planet.

Having been thoroughly briefed by our scientific team, on both the genetic situation and the proposed action, we mobilised ourselves somewhat reluctantly for our task. Using our various technologies (which were quite considerably in advance of the technologies which humanity possesses even today) to move swiftly around the planet, we broadcast messages to communities as we found them, calling them together, to carry out this work as quickly as possible. We did our best to conduct ourselves honourably, and to provide support and comfort to our human charges, but our activity inevitably caused a degree of fear amongst the native humans. Of course, the technologies we had were completely unknown to these still-new beings, and must have impressed them hugely as we whizzed around the skies, spoke to them in booming voices the like of which they had never heard, and despatched the unfortunate half-breed atrocities from a distance, painlessly and from their point of view, with consummate ease.

As a result of all this impressive activity we were inevitably deified by these very inexperienced young humans, who were now always going to be in awe and fright of us, whatever we did to recover the situation.

We were recorded by the verbal traditions of the time, to feature in many later mythologies. In one such mythology (the Greek), my commanding officer became that being later known as Zeus. I, because of my communication and energy-related skills was more of a favourite amongst humans than many of the others. Because of my communications role, I was relieved from the task of killing off the malformed half-breed man-animals, and perhaps because of this was seen in a more kindly light. But I too was deified as the being who was later known by the Greeks as Hermes. There were to be other such names for crew members that would appear later in mythologies in many parts of the planet.

The task was eventually completed. The genetic coding of the humans was further modified, by the spreading of a "designer disease" which effectively changed the DNA. The altered human beings continued on their journey, and their cycle of re-incarnations through many short lives (relative to our own) and broadly, all seemed to be well. We and the spaceship were to return many, many times, and were to be widely seen on earth, performing our monitoring and caretaking roles, so that multiple generations of the developing humans experienced us at different times of their lives.

Many of these sightings were to be embedded in stories passed down from father to son with great care, across many generations. Way in the future, these stories were to become part of the many mythologies of emerging cultures all over the planet!

Looking back on this dream, I see that it appears as fact: and, although it was an event that took place while I was sleeping, this is how I experienced it. I could never be sure about which elements were indeed true, but this oft-repeated dream was extremely realistic and I was deeply involved in it, not just an observer. I choose to think that we have these very clear (and often repeating) 'reality' dreams as a result of distant memories of something which really happened in a much earlier incarnation and at another level of frequency, and which we are supposed to remember – for whatever reason...

There was a sting in all of this: there was a shock of recognition in store for me, but it was not to be delivered until some fifteen years later:

SPACE CAPTAIN RETURNS

At that time in my business life, I had set up a leading edge Computer Graphics Bureau, and was looking for a marketing director for the project. I had arranged an appointment with a candidate who seemed well-qualified and suitable, and was extremely pleasant (and who somehow appeared familiar) over the phone, so that I was actually looking forward to his visit to our offices. At the appointed time, who should walk into my office but...my commanding officer, from that epic and oft-repeated dream of fifteen years (and God alone knows how many centuries) earlier! I was shocked to the core as I recognised him and it took me quite a few moments to regain my composure.

We never spoke of this. How could I credibly explain any of this to a senior member of my staff in this, the real world, without being thought completely mad – or so I rationalised to myself! But he was the same warm and genial man I had experienced on the spaceship,

still needing my continuing support, and yet, with that support in place, very effective at what he was doing. In fact, in so many aspects our relationship was an unnerving duplication of my 'reality dream' of our past interaction!

The contact was to end sadly and dramatically. After two years we sold the business and I was never to see him, my ex-commanding officer and now business chum again. His constant generosity of spirit meant that far too many people had taken advantage of him and a few months after we parted, I heard that his life, always in turmoil, had become too much for him to continue. One afternoon, he was found dead in his car, by the roadside at a favourite beauty spot. Sadly, he had committed suicide by taking an overdose, and left the planet. I hope for his sake it was a peaceful exit, and a happy release from his difficult life here.

Just one more thing. Over the years since this incident, I have spotted several people who, I could swear, were also with me on the bridge of that great space vessel that featured in those vivid dreams I experienced twenty years earlier, and from aeons of time back. Some mythological stories indicate that some of the advanced beings who were visitors to this planet, became trapped in its density. Perhaps this is what befell our whole crew, and as a result, we have been here ever since, reincarnating with the rest of humanity. Whatever the truth of it, the impression I have is that the team from that great time ago is reassembling here, for some purpose that none of us yet know.

I wonder when it will be revealed, and indeed, what it might be?

It appears to me that there are many memories that humanity continues to hold collectively, about this and other ancient events, which are now consigned by most of us to be *mythology*. Of all of these the phenomenon of Atlantis seems to me to be the most important. No other ancient civilisation from beyond recorded history looms as large as does this story of two high technology societies, with deep differences in philosophy, and the resulting competition between them. It is important to say that there are many, many differing views about Atlantis. Everyone with half an interest has their own pet theory, mythology or explanation!

The geography of our entire planet appears to have radically changed since Atlantis, and the great argument about where it physically existed will probably never be settled. Indeed, one of the theories we have examined is that Atlantis was both the civilisation, and the earth grid that supported it (as explained in Chapters 8 and 9). And, rather like the British Empire in far more recent times, Atlantis appears to have had many colonies, some of which were very substantial, all over the planet; all of whom might justifiably have called themselves 'Atlantis'. This leads me to speculate that perhaps all the location claims are, to some extent, true.

Years after the final act of 'The Space Captain' adventure I was to have a channelled discussion about Atlantis. Here, we talk with the being Altazar, who on a previous occasion told us that he, unlike Quazar, had many incarnations on Earth, in human form. In this channelling of a couple of years ago, he talks about the history of Atlantis, coming up with information which I know may cause great disagreement amongst the 'cognoscenti' of Atlantis. But he has one advantage: he was there in his previous life, and still has all those memories intact...albeit that he conveys it from his own energy and past life perspective.

Peter: *Altazar, I have received some questions from someone outside this group who wishes to know about the history of Atlantis. I think that there is much here which is revealing for us. We would be very grateful if you could shed some light on what really happened there.*

Altazar: *It would be my pleasure.*

Peter: *We understand that there was a philosophical difference that ended in a war between Atlantis and Lemuria. Can you tell us if this is true, and what actually happened?*

Altazar: *This was not a war in the sense that you have wars so unfortunately on this planet today. It was an occasion when the Atlanteans were working in part on new technology. The Lemurians, being of a very different spiritual and philosophical inclination, visited the Atlanteans frequently, and attempted to persuade them to desist. They were not killing each other, physically speaking. However, they used their psychic powers to attempt to change each others' ways of thinking on these subjects.*

Meanwhile, the technological developments continued, and the Lemurians then worked psychically to damage the experimental work that was being done by those parts of the Atlantean race who were committed to the technological solutions.

The Lemurians through their own selfish egoness, and believing that they were right and the others were wrong, interfered. Through their interfering in a way which they believed (as you have been discussing with Quazar) was for the good of the planet and the light, in their self-righteousness, they interfered with the work that was being done by the Atlanteans.

This work was, in its own right, of the light, and was, in its own way, moving forward the races of the planet. However, it was also work that needed to be developed lovingly. That was the situation until the psychic interruptions. Then everything was kicked out of kilter.

So here in an interesting concept. 'Warfare' in Atlantis was mostly a matter of intellectual competition and sabotage. It was not, in the early stages, about physical battle at all. To continue:

Peter: *What, then, was the nature of this work?*

Altazar: *This work, as you are aware, was the development of crystal-based technologies to communicate physically, mentally, emotionally, spiritually. Not only with beings incarnate on earth, but also with beings from other places, and also the sources of energy in other places. For both time travel, and for other travel in the physical ways, between planets and star-systems as well as across the planet.*

Peter: *When this system was damaged, and presumably it was operating when it was damaged, what was the result of the interference?*

Altazar: *There were great magnetic earth waves which were set off, explosions on the planetary surface and the interior. You see, they were working with energies that they did not really understand yet – particularly as they were now themselves working out of ego, to prove themselves right and the others wrong. So their views were distorted, and their work became distorted. It is* a sad moment in the earth's development, with its human race.

Peter: We understand that the tectonic plates of the earth were fractured, that major earthquakes followed, and that this is what caused the disappearance of Atlantis. Is this also true?

Altazar: This is true. The electromagnetic movements caused a series of eruptions, and great damage. As you say, Atlantis disappeared.

Peter: Can you tell us, in terms of current geography, where Atlantis was located?

Altazar: Well, the American philosophers and speakers like to think that it is under the Pacific ocean, while Europeans place it under the Atlantic. However, it really was a movement away from there, and now what is left has moved a great distance, and is what today you call Siberia. The core of it did not go underneath the earth or the sea in the way which you now believe, although parts of the periphery are there still, to mislead you.

Peter: So what was the fate of Atlantis, if present day Siberia is in some way the remains of it?

Altazar: Well, the explosions on the land were to wipe out all the race that remained at that time. Many had escaped, of course, in different vehicles and travelling in parties from Atlantis: and found themselves in safer places.

Peter: Was the polarity of the earth the same as it is now, or has there been a major polar shift?

Altazar: The polar shift has been significant by at least 15 degrees.

Peter: So that, while we see Siberia today as a place of great temperature extremes, was that perhaps different at that time?

Altazar: *The part of Siberia that was Atlantis was in a much warmer climate than it is today.*

Peter: *Can you identify that part?*

Altazar: *That part is close to Lake Baical, as it is known today.*

I have to say this claim by Altazar is totally out of line with current, mainstream thinking. Nevertheless, I get the impression that he is totally confident about this information!

Peter: *Thank you. And where was Lemuria located?*

Altazar: *Lemuria was located on the other end of the land mass in the southern part of Asia, where you now have the Easter islands. This is approximately the area of which we speak. The land masses were quite different in those days.*

Peter: *So you are saying that the total geography of the earth has shifted a great deal?*

Altazar: *Indeed, yes. What was land became water, and what was covered with water became land – of course, I exaggerate, but it was a great change.*

Peter: *Thank you. What happened to the people that survived Atlantis? And do we have the remains of those people in groups that we would recognise now, or have they integrated fully?*

Altazar: *They were the seeds for many different races. The Pharaohs of Egypt, their wisdom came from Atlantis. They were keepers of the Atlantean magic in relation to incarnation, art and the understanding of metaphysics, the star systems, knowledge of other beings in other dimensions and communication with them. And on earth, beings such as Shiva, Krishna also held this knowledge. Theirs was the final opportunity the*

Atlanteans had to show and disseminate their 'magic' as perceived by the other human beings living in the area which was to become India.

Peter: What about the great ancient civilisations in South America? Are they related?

Altazar: Indeed. They too, were related. Of course, the land mass was different, and there were beings who lived among that land who brought the Atlanteans and the Atlantean way into their life-forms, and introduced the understanding, particularly of sound and music as a communication vehicle with other beings from other places. Finally, the Atlanteans who went east found themselves in the land masses that became China. This was limited at this time, to the area you know as Peking. They were a developing race based on a combination of Lemurian and Atlantean cultures.

Peter: What of the great mystical traditions of Tibet?

Altazar: Tibet's powerful traditions evolved later from a Lemurian group that went through the Indian land mass. They chose a different route, a far more spiritually, philosophically based route.

Peter: Thank you. Can you tell us how long ago was the demise of Atlantis in our terms?

Altazar: In your terms it was approximately eight thousand years ago.

Peter: So, in terms of our history this is relatively recent?

Altazar: Indeed, this is why this is well known to you.

Peter: Well, thank you for that description, it really is in many respects radically different from the view that is held here currently.

Altazar: There are many views of this, because, as we have attempted to show you many times, if you *asked a random sample of human beings in your country to explain what was occurring in Yugoslavia, and why this damage, carnage, has occurred, and what is the outcome, you would get many disparate and ill-informed views.*

Peter: *So you are saying that the topic of Atlantis is similar in this respect?*

Altazar: *Indeed, many well-intentioned people have their belief systems about what happened, indeed, many who were there at the time also have different beliefs about what the problem was, as you would imagine would be the case, with the polarity and judgement that was present among those people at that time. There were few there who were truly of the light.*

We now move on to look at the interaction, and flow, between some of the great civilisations of the past:

Lorcan: *Altazar, you spoke a moment ago of some of the South American cultures. Could you be more specific about where some of the South American civilisations lay, and who were the representatives of that. I am under the impression that some of these great civilisations came before the culture known as India. I would like some clarity in terms of your viewpoint, because it has been indicated to me that some of these South American civilisations came after Atlantis and Lemuria. Can you elaborate?*

Altazar: *Indeed, you are now having to understand the waxing and waning of civilisations. The civilisations in the area of South America as it is now, were well developed at the time of the damage that was created by the Lemurian/*

Atlantean conflagration. They, therefore, were less severely influenced by the arrival of the Atlanteans in their midst. Indeed, they embraced them with love, as would be the expectation of any civilisation as advanced as theirs, and they already were, well developed.

The other aspect is that their civilisation did not wane over the next thousands of years in the way that the other civilisations waned. So, although Krishna and Shiva were to become the mythological figures in India, the presence of energies and beings from Atlantis in the Mayan civilisation was not inculcated in mythology, but rather kept in very 'alive' ways – they were present because the civilisation sustained its life, and did not degenerate into mythological memories. Whereas in India, it was some more thousands of years before that civilisation really grew to the fullness of its strengths, and beauty, and abundance, by which time Shiva and Krishna were history, mythologically speaking.

This next section deals with an important message: how we might draw on lessons, experiences and technology taken from what we have done in the past (by which I mean in our earlier lives), to help us to find new ways of being in the current era. In this context, it would appear that the fall of Atlantis caused the seeding of several major civilisations that are a part of our recorded history, albeit very early on, and their connection with our modern world can still be understood. The demise of Atlantis also appears to have been a lengthy process, and not just a single event. It was after most of the process was complete, before any real warfare, in the modern sense, was to take place.

Gwen: *Many people today tend to hark back to the past, perhaps studying some of the workings of Atlantean crystal technology, as well as the native American culture and their way of seeing things. Should we not be taking the essence of some of that experience to move forward, rather than going back? Is there not a fresh approach to the use of crystals and of being in touch with the earth, new rituals, perhaps?*

Altazar: *It is of course possible for human beings, to design, invent and find ways to live on this Earth with great spiritual honour. And those who choose to make it their work during this lifetime to understand and recapture and learn many of the sophisticated traditions developed by previous civilisations are, in so doing, assisting the learning process; when they do it, not from a place of 'we are right and they are wrong' but rather 'how can we learn the essence of their work so that we can develop an essence which is true for humanity at this stage of its evolution, at this place and in this time?'*

So we agree with you. It is the case with great mathematicians, for example, some are born great and others become great because of their diligent study, and their understanding of those who have worked before them. So a leap into greatness might not be the quickest way forward for every human being; each has to follow his own path. It is through understanding, through harnessing the emotion of romanticism and sentimentality towards the past, which is part of the human condition. In harnessing this, people who might not otherwise awaken to possibilities for living on the earth harmoniously are awakened to do so through their sentimentality. Then, as they do so, with the enquiring, creative, spiritual connections and mind of the human being, they will adapt to ways that will be suitable for the twenty-first century.

Lorcan: *Altazar, regarding the contribution of the Celtic civilisations, how can we adapt to Celtic rites of passage at this time? We are sitting in a land which is rich with information from the past, but that seems not to be easily accessible.*

Altazar: *I am not an expert in the Celtic tradition, any more than I am an expert in any tradition. However, you will find more knowledge of the Celtic traditions if you go to the parts of this land where those traditions died out more recently. You will learn from those around you how long ago it was that this part of this country had true Celts practising their law. So we must look elsewhere for the understanding. Remember, it was a law that was the way for people many hundreds of thousands of years ago, and would of course not all be appropriate today. There is wisdom in there, especially in the area of mathematics, the sacred geometry of the designs of the Celts and yet you need not be seduced by this. It is only indicative of what may be possible in the twenty-first century. You will need to apply great creativity and lateral thinking to take the Celtic information and then transform it for modern day use.*

So all these ancient traditions have steadily built towards what we are today. And by looking at the great achievements of past civilisations, we can see that humanity as a whole is on a journey, and continues to evolve – even more rapidly at the present time!

GROWTH AND DEVELOPMENT

You grew
From much
        to even more –
There is no door
You need to close:
You chose your path
      to this
From that:
Rejecting
     is no part of your directing.

Do not give in –
Give out
      some
Of what you've taken in –
Don't cry too long:
It is just one device
To sing well your life's song.

Chapter Five

Time And The Fall Of Humanity

THE NATURE OF TIME

Moving nearer
Earth-existence
The distance between Problem-and-Solution
Widens,
      Cause-and-Effect
Are pulled apart
When everywhere out there
     the pair
Is one:
     has not
        what is begun within-without
Thereby come without a doubt
To be?

     It is
Our seeing it
Depends on time –
       that magnifying glass
    of what takes place
    in the living space
Of ever growing-knowing.

How else can it replace
     its past and present splendour
With still more blazing grace!

We humans think of time as a strictly serial event. Each minute follows the last with a measured and reliable solidarity – one of the few things that can be relied upon absolutely, on this planet. Albert Einstein spent much of his life studying the nature of time. His conclusion, quite contrary to public conviction, was that time is a series of parallels, and in some way, all human experience might be happening simultaneously!

However, even if time is structured quite differently to what we expect, we experience it as happening serially. In this respect, the great Mayan civilisation had a sacred calendar that spans a cycle of 26,000 years. Embedded in it is great and highly accurate knowledge of cosmology, the movement of planets and star systems in relation to Earth. The cycle is very close to its ending, and a new cycle is projected to commence very early in the new century. With this event a series of happening are predicted, not only by the Maya, but by many ancient cultures. The expectation is that the end of this galactic cycle will bring with it a miraculous transition of the Earth and of humanity.

This idea is further complicated by the fact that there seem to be many dimensions of existence apart from ours, and that beings in other dimensions have a quite different experience of time to ours. In some cases, they are apparently outside time as we understand it. Yet it appears that they are all, to some extent, being affected by what is now happening to the Earth.

Time, and what is happening as a result of the ending of a major cycle, is a subject worthy of exploration. One of our first discussions on this topic was with a being called Antiguana, on September 20th 1994. We had originally met Antiguana when we had explored some information about sacred architecture. We had been told that she was the being who had advised both Plato and Pythagorus! Compelling credentials!

Peter: Antiguana, in human experience time has always been taken as a serial event and experience, and yet recently we have been told that this is not the case, that there is a quite different dimensionality to time. We would like to explore this phenomenon with you, to understand it rather better than we do at the moment. Perhaps you can talk about this subject in general to start with?

Antig: Time is a phenomenon that has been invented to allow your human minds to accommodate your experience on earth. As you know, you have free will, and yet you have no memory of the future at all – this is part of the experience of being human, with which you are familiar. You do not ever know the outcome of your actions, except to the extent that you have observed those actions and their effects in the past. This limits your ability, and your sensitivity to the future, and you cannot be so responsible for your actions in the way that beings of consciousness and light are responsible for past and future and present simultaneously.

   This is the nature of human existence and this is what makes it such an exciting challenge for all who enter into the three-dimensional form. The fourth dimension of time is the way that this is now calibrated, managed for your three-dimensional brains to conceptualise the framework in which they have to operate. It is a limited concept because all matter, existence, opportunities, challenges and actions are simultaneously present at any moment in multi-dimensional form. They all exist. However, we choose which way we move within that framework.

Peter: We have a very small percentage of the population who are regarded as prophets, seers, *perhaps fortune tellers: people who in different spheres have some ability to predict what we call the future. Can you comment on that?*

Antig: *This is not in integrity with the human condition. If you knew what would happen next you would break the rules of the framework in which you have chosen to operate. So it is not acceptable to predict the future and those who do so only see one of many futures, since there are many possible outcomes. You choose your own outcome through your processes of manifestation. When you ask someone to advise you on the outcomes, you are actually manifesting your future, or they are doing it for you and you are giving away your power.*

Peter: *So any attempt at prophecy is in fact a manipulation?*

Antig: *Indeed. This is manipulating human minds to create a future for themselves by telling them what will happen, and if they believe it then they will make that happen. It is the most crude form of auto-suggestion and manifestation.*

Peter: *Which beings were responsible for setting out time as we understand it for humanity?*

Antig: *This was such a long time ago and yet it is part of the all-present universe at all times. There is no individual responsible as you would understand it. It was the highest realms of the godhead that created earth and set its framework for all time.*

Peter: *That suggests to me that time, even though we regard as limiting, is also a sacred structure.*

Antig: *Indeed, we would never indicate anything other. It is the most sacred of structures as it does enable the soul to truly develop.*

Peter: *We are told that time as it is experienced is now coming to an end and this is supported by* discoveries like the Mayan calendar which predicts an ending to time. Is this to be taken as truth or is it simply a misunderstanding of the mechanical nature of time?

Antig: This is a misunderstanding. It is merely a completion of one phase of the framework, and the human souls as they now evolve and develop begin to appreciate the multi-dimensionality of the universe, and so move into a new framework that will have its own time framework as you have always had on this planet in these dimensions.

Peter: If we move as it were into a new time cycle, does this new time have added dimensionality compared with what we have experienced up to now?

Antig: It is the way it is for all time.

Peter: I take your answer to be that, no, time doesn't have any other dimension.

Antig: That is correct.

Peter: Are we capable of moving beyond that concept of time or are we bound to it in perpetuity?

Antig: You choose to come into a world where the framework is that you do not know what is to come next. That is the framework you come into and time is part of the structure that permits this to be.

Peter: So it's a structure to enable us to explore?

Antig: It is a necessary condition for the being not to experience the future before it occurs. Without it you would not have the human experience.

Peter: Yes, that makes sense.

Antig: So it is not just a pretty concept dreamed up to create some experiment; it is a necessary condition like the atmosphere is an experiment. You are most fortunate to have this because there is tremendous opportunity to create your own destiny. You do not see the future and so you truly have free will; in the way that we have not got free will as you conceive it and know it. Treasure and relish the most sacred of opportunities for the human spirit to have true free will.

Peter: Thank you, that gives me a completely new insight into time.

Antig: Your universe is such a benign universe and the creation of earth with such infinite wisdom and joy and delightful dimensionality is really one of the wonders of this universe.

Peter: It is suggested that some humans are capable of time travel. The references are so frequent, it must I think, refer to some phenomenon we are not generally aware of. Can you explain that for us ?

Antig: Well of course, any being in the universe may travel through time; the question is whether you wish to break the sacred lock into which you have entered. This is like agreeing to play a game of football and then playing the game off the pitch.

Peter: Are there humans that have broken the rules ?

Antig: Many have attempted this and of course many have achieved it, I wish to be clear it is both of these that I speak of, and in doing so they have broken their sacred promises.

Peter: Is there a point in human experiences where a human being passes out of time as we know it?

Antig: You see not what we speak of clearly yet. You choose as a soul to come into this framework. You know that time is a construct and you choose to play the game and be totally absorbed in the game, just as in a game of football, knowing that it is only a game and the rules are constructed for the game to be played. You see souls may remember that time is not a reality of the universe. When they remember, they can access that knowingness, and *yet choose to play this game to be stretched and developed with the opportunities that this world offers them as souls, by playing the game within time's framework.*

Peter: *Our experience of time is very different from how it appeared only a few years ago; as if time is becoming much more compacted. I would very much like to hear your perspective on that as well.*

Antig: *This is an illusion you are all experiencing. The rate of change of your environment is now so fast that you misinterpret the high degree of activity that you expect to complete in a day as being an indication that the day is actually changed. This is all part of the human perception of time which in its own way does tend to limit its experience.*

This information gave me a great deal to work with, but I did not really understand the basic principles articulated above until almost a year later. On this occasion I had, of all things, a telepathic discussion on the very same subject, while on a crowded train. By the end of this communication, I really felt that I knew what Einstein had been on about...

TIME IS NOT THE FOURTH DIMENSION

Wednesday 23rd August 1995. I am on a train, going into London (about a 35 minute journey), and minding my own business, when SURPRISE – I start to have what turns out to be quite a lengthy telepathic communication. Of all things, its about the nature of time. Although there was no formal 'announcement', I identified this communication to me as coming from a 'messenger' i.e. a discarnate being, but speaking quite clearly into my head. Moreover, this being was in some

way familiar to me; I was sure I recognized the 'signature' as something remembered dimly!

"Think of your first life on Earth", the messenger said, "as being like an interactive video. A journey where the main relationships, challenges and scenarios are set by you before you incarnated, a bit like choosing the 'degree of difficulty'...When you arrive in your new human body, you completely forget all that went before, and from there, the choices and responses that you make during the journey determine the outcome of your present life."

Wow!...or was it?

...Well, on reflection this idea seemed quite familiar: I had little difficulty with what, after a moment, seemed a simple enough concept. I had come across a similar idea before, which stated that between our many incarnations, we go to a place of 'rest and review', to look back on the life just completed, and evaluate it. The final part of this process was apparently to agree, and set up the major elements of our next life – new challenges and parameters against which these would be played out. Key events and relationships would figure prominently here!

"Ah," said the messenger seeing that I had made a mental connection, "now we will use this metaphor of the video to illustrate something *far* more important..."

"Eh, what's going on??" my left brain seemed to say...

"Be quiet. Just listen!" came the command from my right brain...

I settled down. This might take a while!

Clickety-clack, clickety clack, went the rails in the background with a kind of comforting monotony.

"One of humanity's fundamental assumptions about the nature of things is incorrect," said the voice, "and it prevents you from a higher understanding of how things really are..."

"Please explain," said my head valiantly, the rest of me feeling somewhat bemused.

"Well, we wish you to understand that time is not the fourth dimension," came the somewhat mystifying response.

Now, *there* is a stunning idea!

"If time is not the fourth dimension," said my brain (left and right sections in harmony for once) "then what is?" The messenger really had my attention now!

"The fourth dimension is frequency."

Well, this made no sense at all. I must have communicated that thought immediately, for the messenger went on to explain patiently, "Let us use the metaphor of the interactive video, representing the journey of one lifetime, to help explain... Let us say that your first life is run at a frequency of 6000 – it really does not matter about the units of measurement, except that they are comparative."

"Well, OK..." I say, somewhat lamely and hesitantly.

"Now, on frequency 6000, your life is being played out, say, every ten frames: that is, presenting you with another snapshot at high speed, on every tenth frame...1,11,21,31,41,51,61 and so on, ad infinitum. Your brain then synthesizes the frames, giving you a continuous experience."

"Like viewing a film?" I'm a quick learner!

"Yes...well done!" The response was rather like that of a proud parent encouraging its young child.

"So we are in a sort of virtual reality?" I was beginning to enjoy this.

"A somewhat limited concept, but it will do," came the distinctly tart reply; this being wasn't going to allow me to get too cocky!

Well, I can handle all of that, I think...

"...and your choices and responses, made along the way, might take you onto another track at the same frequency: for example 62,72,82,92,102,and this would be a different set of experiences, determined by your free will, OK?" I was really being pushed along here!

"OK!" I said.

"Well, for the purpose of what we want to tell you, this illustration will do, although in practice there are vastly more options than just ten tracks."

"So, I conduct a life at one frequency, and there are many potential tracks at that same frequency. My choices, made along the way, determine which track I am on at any one time." This connection came easily.

"Now," said the messenger, "we will illustrate how time is not a dimension, but a sacred structure caused by the interaction of the real fourth dimension, (which is frequency), and the spiral of re-incarnation..."

"Huh!" came my involuntary response...this one had me fazed. "How am I supposed to get my head around that one?" Just when my own cleverness was beginning to impress me!

"So, let us take your second life..."

"Assuming re-incarnation?" I wasn't going to let him have it all his own way!

"Yes, yes...Well, the second life could not play out at frequency 6000, it would keep coming into conjunction with the first as you changed tracks. This is potentially very confusing for a three-dimensional being..."

"Er, yes...I think I follow..." I was now having to try hard to keep up.

"In order to give you a wide choice of frequencies to work in and through, and the potential for many lives in the physical dimensions of your planet, you humans are subjected to what your Bible calls 'The Fall'..."

The messenger paused to let that sink in and went on to say, "What happens is that you steadily ratchet downwards through the available frequencies..."

"What...?" I was getting lost again.

"Well, imagine that your second life-video is played out at frequency 5900, to avoid confusing it with the first, at 6000..." This messenger was good, I was really beginning to get it..."And the next life is at 5800, and the next at 5700, and so on."

"Oh yes, I can see that"...and I could!

"Of course," said the messenger, "by progressing this way, you have the appearance of moving through time – but actually it is a sacred structure, caused by ratcheting down through the frequencies. What your Bible calls 'The Fall' is absolutely necessary for this experience. The interaction of frequency and the ratcheting process causes this experience you call time; it is actually quite mechanical in many respects."

"But then," I think, "wouldn't we run out of time eventually...?"

"Very good! I think he is getting it," the messenger appears to say to some third party observer...and then back to me, "have you heard of the Mayan Calendar?"

"Yes, doesn't it predict the complete ending of time? Quite soon?" This seems a bit dire to me; everything coming to a halt, just like that...

"No – you are still thinking of time as a dimension, and if a necessary dimension were to end, yes, there would be great trouble. But we are merely talking about the ending of this particular sacred structure, which allows you incarnated beings to explore the physical world you are in. The Cosmos, too, has its time, but it's...well, it's just different. It, too, is a sacred structure to allow a different level of consciousness to explore different dimensions."

"OK, but why would you do that?" I asked, thinking that this whole cosmic exercise might just be a little pointless. "What is the point of this – what did you call it – sacred structure?"

Clickety-clack, clickety-clack drones on in the background, as soothing as a repeated lullaby.

The messenger now seemed to direct an intense beam of energy straight at me, in an effort to hold and focus my attention.

"Well, we in our world are multi-dimensional beings, without the kind of time that you experience. Because of this, we always know the outcome of every action or decision we take, immediately, as we take it. Cause and effect are, for us, simultaneous. This arrangement serves us well, but it does not provide a basis for exploring, let us say, a new dimension."

I think, "Well, I can see that you might not have much curiosity, if you always knew the answer as you asked the question...seems a mite tedious, now that I think about it."

"Quite so...do you see now, how the idea of serial time, in the way you experience it is so valuable? As you don't really know what the outcome will be from any one action, humanity as a whole tries every conceivable option on its journey forward?"

In a flash, I see another angle. "Does this mean that we are at some kind of unexplored frontier?"

Clickety-clack...

"Well," comes the messenger's thought, "remember, first, that all this experience is actually more like a parallel process than the serial way you perceive it. All your many lives are, from our perspective, happening simultaneously..."

My perspective, however, does not grasp that very well.

The messenger continues, "Universal Consciousness, God, to use the Human term, is continually spreading the bounds of experience. In your terms, He likes to explore and occupy new dimensions.

You are all acting as probes, into this 'frontier' of the physical world. Part of what you do is to relay your experiences back to the centre of all things."

"Well then, if we are running out of time, what will happen to humanity?" This question quite suddenly becomes the focal point of this discussion.

"Many of you will choose to stay in this physical dimension, but in your future you will start to experience it differently. You will return soon to multi-dimensionality. The many powerful faculties you had in your past, were suppressed in order to allow you to explore through the sacred and mechanical structure of time. Soon, all these faculties will be returned to you. You will once more become multi-dimensional creatures, with powers that today would look to you like the powers of Gods – which indeed, they are..."

"Wow!" I suddenly get this amazing vision of...

"THE TRAIN NOW ARRIVING AT PLATFORM TWO IS THE STOPPING TRAIN, ALL STATIONS FROM KINGSTON. WE APOLOGISE FOR ANY DELAY IN YOUR JOURNEY..."

Instantly, the platform announcement snaps me out of my reverie – I realise that we are here! We have arrived at the end of our journey. Time to get off the track we have been on, to change to a faster line...!

No more training – perhaps now we can fly!

THE TRAIN NOW STANDING ON PLATFORM THREE IS THE THROUGH TRAIN TO...?

YOU HAVE THE TIME YOU NEED!

Rushing
Crushes Time
Until the hours
       no longer rhyme
And we can't hear
The music of earth's atmosphere.
    Indeed
We no more know,
       cannot believe
It sings
Than angels grasp
We have no wings!

Rushing
     shrinks,
Condenses time
Until Cause and Effect
Run into one
     or fall apart
So they can no more play
Throwing the ball to one another,
To entertain us
    on our arduous climb
To ever higher reaches
Of the sublime.

Chapter Six

Some Latent Human Powers

As suggested by the last chapter, it is my belief that we humans have a wide variety of latent powers; extremely powerful faculties outside what we regard as the norm. The present situation on our planet is one of rapidly increasing energies around us. One of the effects of this, coming at the very end of the present time cycle, is to start reconnecting us with these powers – part of a remarkable metamorphosis that each of us can now choose to experience. And these powers are starting, oh so tentatively for most of us, to show up right now!

I have been privileged to have had some of these powers demonstrated to me at first hand! The following stories demonstrate phenomena which I believe will be within our grasp in the foreseeable future; not just at will, but fully integrated into what human beings are starting to become. They will be part of an automatic faculty!

The first incident was a most dramatic demonstration of teleporting; moving from one place to another in an instant, transported merely by thought!

TIME FOR TEA

As mentioned elsewhere in these stories, we – my partner Oonagh and I – live in a beautiful and unusual property on the edge of the river Thames. On one side of a reasonable-sized lawn there is a wet-dock, in which sits the eighty-foot houseboat we live in. On the other side there is an 1880s boathouse, which functions as the office and hub of operations from which our various activities are conducted. The two are about a hundred feet apart. This distance is crucial to this next story...

This tale involves our clairvoyant friend John Frank. Like many of our experiences with him, this one too is out of the ordinary! In this case, as on many previous occasions, I was working with John and I happened to ask his Committee – a group of five discarnate energy beings who he works with clairvoyantly – if it was true that some human beings could teleport. This phenomenon intrigued me enormously...

"Oh, yes," they told me. "This is a capability which a few very special humans have learnt to use, although you all possess the latent ability to do this".

I expressed amazement and some confusion. I just couldn't imagine moving from one place to another in a fraction of a second. We talked about it for a while.

Eventually, the Committee said "Would you like us to provide a demonstration for you in the next few days?"

As I have learnt time and time again, there is certainly nothing quite so convincing as a practical demonstration of an ability which tests one's disbelief! "Wonderful!" I exclaimed. There was no sensation of concern; I was totally filled with enthusiasm, "I would be really interested to do that,"...and then promptly, (as so often seems to happen with me) over the next few hours, I forgot the conversation entirely!

A few days later we had truly atrocious weather. I was working in the office, which has lovely views, but no kitchen or toilet facilities. Normally this is no great problem, as I simply cross from the boathouse to the houseboat using the path around the lawn which connects the two, when the need arises.

However, on this particular morning it was literally pouring with rain outside; not just ordinarily heavy rain but that tropical, vertical rain that I often think of as 'stair rods'. In fact, on reflection, it was quite the heaviest rainfall that I can remember. It was definitely the kind of rain where, if I had been out in it, even for a few moments, I would have been soaked to the skin, and every item of my clothing wringing wet.

After having worked hard for most of the morning –
I had been writing a report on the findings from a
recent business trip to Russia, for a consulting client –
I was distinctly thirsty. I needed a break from the
rather heavy report, and I decided to make myself a
large cup of good, English tea.

Shortly after this decision, I was in our kitchen on
the top floor of our 'double-decker' houseboat, on the
other side of the lawn from the office, carrying out this
decision and going about the everyday task of putting
the kettle on and fixing my tea. All of a sudden I did
the most momentous doubletake. Realisation hit me
like a ton of bricks.

*I was making tea here, in the other part of the
property. There was no way in this torrential rain that I
could have crossed the lawn without getting completely
soaked and yet I was still totally dry.*

I was understandably agitated, indeed, I was
astonished. How could this possibly be? The rainstorm
had not broken for hours. I know that sometimes I
switch off while I do day-to-day things, but in this
weather what I had just experienced, and the
realisation that followed, was quite impossible...

It was only then that I remembered the Committee's
offer of a demonstration...!

The subject of telepathy features at several points in this
book. I believe that this faculty alone has the power to
totally change who and what we are. I have had a number
of telepathic experiences, but they are for me, still rarities;
most days pass for me without any conscious telepathic
communication. The beings we talk with in channelling say
we can work with them telepathically. In the following
extracts from various channelled conversations we examine
how this possibility might be opened up:

Peter: We have been told and we read from other
channellings that the technique of channelling
will fairly soon become something that we
don't need, as we can develop a much more
telepathic connection with you and others in
your realm; a conscious telepathic connection.
I would like your guidance on this phenomena,
and how we might move towards it, what steps
we might take.

Arcturus: Indeed, you are well on the route to
developing these faculties already; all of you.
The experience of sitting in this process
participating in channelling work, whether you
are the speaker or one of the channels is
irrelevant. It is all a process of learning to be
sensitive to our energies and this is one of the
best ways, learning by experience, for each of
you to be more effective and open up your own
channels. In time you will not need to have
verbal channelling present for you, but for
now it is part of the learning curve.

Peter: I know beings of the non-physical worlds
and dimensions will not normally act unless
they are invited to do so and therefore the
following may seem a strange statement: I
would like to request and invite you to be in
telepathic communication with us. Does the
fact of this request make a difference?

Arcturus: This makes an enormous difference because
it opens up the receptors of your own cells.
You see, what you are doing, technically
speaking, is commanding yourselves to be
receiving, so that, in turn, the receptors will be
open and capable of receiving. Of course, they
are capable of receiving even when they are

not so commanded, but they do not automatically line up to receive.

Peter: *Arcturus, I formally invite you specifically, and other beings of the light who are working with me and with those around me to be in direct telepathic communication, and I command my cells to open up and align to all such communication, as long as it is from beings of the light who actively support the highest purposes of the ascent of humanity.*

How does that sound to you?

Arcturus: *We have many ways we can practise telepathy, and of course we do not think conventionally in your way. However you need to frame requests effectively, and this is important for you to learn in order that you can manifest all sorts of things. A request is a form which is I request x by x or y or z. Thus 'I request assistance with learning the first steps of telepathic communications. I request a boiled egg on my sandwiches tomorrow... '.*

Ultimately, you will use this capability to communicate with each other more effectively. Right now you may experience some loneliness as you realise how alone you are with this information.

Gwen: *Arcturus, is it your wish that you would like to also communicate telepathically with us?*

Arcturus: *It is more efficient for us, and it takes less energy from us. Also, then we can speak directly into your own models of the world. Each of you has a unique view of how the world works, and when we work through a channel you get an interpretation, albeit wide-ranging, through the channel.*

On an earlier occasion, our friend Neslyn and I had been working with Arcturus, when this subject came up. Here, we discuss the difficulties of telepathic communications between beings who are in vastly different dimensions:

Arcturus: *As you can understand, we can look at a situation which you describe to us in more than one way. It is important to describe your experience to us so that you communicate the situation in your words. We will then actually receive a telepathic communication from you that embraces the words, and also, the brain energies, if you will, around that experience. And in that, we get a complete picture of your experience. Then we can feed back to you what was actually going on energetically. You then have to interpret that in your way, in terms of your physical, emotional, mental and spiritual paradigms as you call them. So now, I hope perhaps you understand that you are beings who have brain and thought patterns etc. and when you communicate telepathically what we see is an energy body.*

Peter: *Can you explain the sense in which is an energy body? Is this a transaction of energy or more than that?*

Arcturus: *We see the form of the energy that is encapsulating your physical form at the time of the communication.*

Peter: *And that is how you would normally see us?*

Arcturus: *That is also what telepathic communication looks like to us. We do not read your words. We read an electromagnetic patterning from your brain which communicates your total energy packaging, which we then receive and we interpret in our own experience. Since we lack your frame of reference in a dimension which integrates the spiritual and physical, we cannot interpret an energetic electromagnetic communication in the way you might think it. Does this make sense?*

Peter: *Yes, it does.*

Arcturus: *I have another metaphor. Let us say you have a thought: 'I would like a banana milkshake'. Well, when this thought is transferred to me telepathically, and you will understand that as I speak through a channel she is offering this particular metaphor for you, when I receive this communication, I receive an energy electromagnetic impulse which is about a wish of yours, although I also have some difficulty in understanding this concept of wishes. I am now interpreting through the channel that you have emotion attached to this 'wish', which, again, I have difficulty interpreting. So what I receive I interpret according to my domain and my frame of reference. For example, I would not understand the channel's metaphor of 'banana milkshake'!*

Peter: *Yes, I think we understand that you are receiving from us an energy package, in which are included many things which we would believe essential to that communication for it to have meaning: and yet the difficulty is that those apparently essential items really have no meaning to you.*

Arcturus: *This is true. This is why we need to be so careful and really understand each other to the extent that is possible through a channel. It is also difficult because she receives the return energy package from me and then puts it in your language, experience and domain, because she cannot communicate to you what my domain is like, because she has not been there or experienced it.*

In our channelling work, we have always been carefully instructed by Quazar about the need for protection, so that there is no unwanted interference in our communication. I asked him if the same techniques need to be applied to telepathic communication, and if so, how to go about it:

Peter: *Should we or can we protect ourselves for telepathy?*

Quazar: *You need to learn a different technology for this. The communication and the energy frequency is quite different. It is human to human. This is absolutely accessible to humans and is less in need of protection than with channelling, because interference is less easy. This is difficult for you to understand...*

Peter: *No, that makes sense to me. My concern is that some of us experience telepathic communication, not just human to human, but with beings in other dimensions. This has the content of channelling, but the methodology of telepathy. I assume this is on a different frequency as well, and maybe that requires specific protection?*

Quazar: *You are, indeed, transmitting telepathically on a different frequency. Telepathy is a connection that occurs through the crown chakra, and the other vortices of chakra energy above the human form, whereas channelling occurs through the chakra at the back of the neck. This is not the same energy, and requires a different form of receiver. Therefore there is more danger in this form of communication, as well, of course, more opportunity.*

With telepathy as you describe it, Peter, you have less problem with interference and you can trust the "cosmic tick"[1] type energy that comes with the telepathic communication you receive. Each of you will have your own energy signature that tells you when your telepathic communications are clear connections into consciousness.

Peter: *Thank you that is really most helpful.*

Towards the end of 1995, as I was beginning to make a great deal of use of E-mail and computer conferencing, I realised that the physical links between various parties on the system also appeared to be facilitating their telepathic ability to communicate. Here, we ask Quazar about this particular phenomenon, which turns out to have aspects of another latent human faculty, that of bi-location:

Peter: *Quazar, I would like to ask a question about the Internet and CompuServe services, which we are using regularly. We have been given the image of this physical network as serving as a substitute for those links that we have lost*

---

[1] A surge of 'electrical' energy I feel over my head and shoulders when I get a strong intuition about something. It appears to me as if someone is verifying that I have got the message accurately!

as a substitute for those links that we have lost or find very difficult, such as our natural power of telepathy. But something additional is happening: several people get the impression that each computer-to-computer link made in the system also acts as a carrier for the personas of those individuals working on it, developing new levels of connectivity between the beings that use it. Can you clarify this for us?

Quazar;   *It has long been possible for the most spiritually evolved on your planet, to bi-locate, as you call it: to choose to be physically present in two places, or more, at once. You all have this capability, however, you have limited yourselves, with your thoughts, to be in only one place at one time.*

However, now you can be in many places at once, when you speak on the telephone, and when you conference call. Now you can conference on your e-mail and be again in many places at the same time. You can learn to send your energy along the lines, so that not only your words are present, but your energy is present where they read your words.

Soon you will understand that the next stage in bi-location is to send a piece of your form, or a spiritual image along the line, with your words and energy. As you do this, each will experience your signature, whatever it may be – a flower, a sun, a raven, a piece of rock – whatever you may choose. And so, eventually (and we say, very, very quickly) you will learn to work without this electronic equipment, because you are, of course, electromagnetic beings and you already have built an energy grid, heart to heart, around the planet, and as that strengthens you will have no need for any wires, cables, fibre optics, or anything else.

Peter: *And did I understand you to say that this will happen now, very, very quickly?*

Quazar: *Indeed; for those more evolved souls, very quickly indeed.*

Peter: *I feel that computer-based systems are more powerful in this respect than the telephone.*

Quazar: *This is true, of course, because they are a more pure form of electro-magnetic carrier.*

Peter: *When you talk of people consciously projecting themselves along this carrier – my impression is, to a large extent, consciously or unconsciously, they are already doing this.*

Quazar: *You have been learning what abilities you have as your technology becomes more and more electric, magnetic rather than mechanical. As you move totally to digital switches throughout, you will find that it gets easier and easier.*

Peter: *There has been a lot of concern about electro-magnetic pollution around us. But it sounds to me as if, apart from being a pollutant, it is also opening up our faculties in some way. Is there some truth in that?*

Quazar: *Well of course, this is what we have been speaking of with you at this time.*

Peter: *I am thinking along much wider lines than the communications systems, including the electricity, the magnetic fields that are generated around us by lighting and circuits and equipment, and televisions; which we are beginning to see as a pollutant.*

Quazar:	*Yes, indeed, they are pollutants and you will not require them for very long.*
Peter:	*None of these systems?*
Quazar:	*You may use them for entertainment, but for pure communication you will find it easier to use your telepathic powers.*
Peter:	*Is there a specific instruction or technique available for us to start to hone these powers, so that they become practically useable?*
Quazar:	*Indeed you can practise communicating with each other through the e-mail, as you call it, and experience passing messages of ever more complexity behind the words.*
Peter:	*Good, and thank you.*

So, if this communication is to be believed, most of the electronic systems we now use will disappear in short order. We shall use telepathy as an everyday form of communication, and develop the ability to bi-locate; that is to project a part of oneself (to start with, a part of one's consciousness) to another location at will. This opens up a whole new range of possibilities such as projecting oneself into animals and birds for instance; remote viewing of places on the planet which are far from your physical location; experiencing past lives, parallel lives, and possible futures. Being human may never be the same again!

Here are two short, but to me most poignant stories about telepathy:

THE AVARICIOUS BEAU

In the late 1980s I had a lady friend, Suzannah, of whom I was very fond, having known her, and her family generally, for some years; in fact John, a friend who had worked with me in a marine business we ran

for a while, was married to one of Suzannah's sisters. However, over time we drifted apart. I knew that she was seeing an acquaintance of mine, Richard, who I knew from the world of yacht racing, which, for a while I had been passionately involved in.

One day, I fell asleep on the train going in to London. I had the most vivid dream of Suzannah coming to me, very upset, to say that she was in terrible trouble. I was so shaken by the dream that, as soon as I arrived home that evening, I called her on the phone, and feeling rather foolish, explained that I had seen her in this dream, and asked if all was well. "Oh yes," she answered breezily, "there's nothing to worry about," and proceeded to chit chat about all sorts of things, making it clear that all was indeed well, and that I was rather 'a silly' to ask her that question. We finished with good wishes on both sides, and I hung up thinking that, for once, my intuitive powers had really let me down!

An hour or so later, Suzannah rang back, clearly in tears. "What on earth is the matter?" I asked. "You were absolutely right," she said. "Actually, I'm really in terrible trouble".

The real story behind her anguish emerged. She told me she and Richard had got engaged, and immediately he had started to harass her about buying a house. He had then persuaded, or more likely bullied her into putting her life savings into a joint bank account...and had promptly gone off with the money! Richard was notoriously unreliable with financial matters, and she knew that the money would never find its way back into their joint account. She was terrified. She did not know what to do, and in particular, she did not know how to break the news to her parents (who had almost certainly warned her about just this eventuality).

It was one of the rare occasions when I have got really angry. I raced around, organising a solicitor, breaking the news (gently) to her parents, and then approached Richard's father, who I happened to have met, and who was actually a very reasonable man. However, I am sure my very terse conversation with him that day, about his errant son, must have appeared like an ultimatum, and pretty severe at that!

Only 48 hours later, all was restored. The money was back in the bank, and needless to say, the engagement was off for good! And Richard had experienced a run-in with his father of monumental proportions, and was distinctly cowed whenever I saw him for the next few weeks.

There was an up-side to this story for me, also. A few months later, Suzannah's parents won the star prize at a charity ball: the use of a huge, luxury yacht in the Mediterranean, for a total of ten guests over a period of two weeks. The prize included the use of a private jet to take the party to the starting point of the cruise on the island of Rhodes, and ferry them back at the end of their stay.

When I was invited to join the party, they made it quite clear that it was in appreciation for services rendered. I really must fall asleep on the train more often!

This was not the first time that such a thing had happened to me. In the early 1980s, when I was seeing my friend Karen, she was in London, and I was working in New York for a two week period; a regular happening at that time in my career. This occurred after I had been there about ten days:

THE RUNAWAY TRUCK

I was away in New York, on work. One particular night I woke up with a start and sat bolt upright, very frightened for Karen's safety. This occurred at approximately 5 am, already mid-morning in the UK. I tried to call her, but there was no reply. Obviously Karen was out of her house.

I called later, evening time in the UK, expressing concern, and was assured that all was well. I thought no more about it, putting it down to a 'worry' dream.

When I got back to London, I rang her, and invited her over. "Well, I would love to," came the reply. "But I really can't." I asked why, and was told she 'had no car'. I questioned her further, and then the truth of the situation I had sensed in New York emerged.

Karen was driving on a dual carriageway road, down a steep hill, on that morning. She came to a set of traffic lights, and was slowing the car down – they were at red – when a large, heavily-laden articulated truck behind her lost its brakes completely!

Out of control, the vehicle crashed into the back of her car, and the force of the impact pushed both of them across the red light and the busy crossing, missing many other vehicles by a miracle. They then accelerated down the hill on the other side of the traffic lights, and as the road swung to the left, demolished the central crash barrier, charged through the oncoming traffic in the opposite lane, and eventually ended up crashing to a standstill in the forecourt of a petrol station. The potential conflagration could have been devastating! Karen's car was unrecognisable, when I went out to see the wreck the following day.

How she had survived uninjured except for a few bruises, I shall never know; that particular guardian

angel did good work that morning! To Karen, it must have seemed like an endless nightmare as this horrific accident was in progress. No wonder her wave of anguish had awakened me, across the Atlantic!

So, it seems that we have the very beginnings of some powers that will, as they come to the fore, completely change what we, as human beings, are. Telepathy is one of the better known possibilities. The ability to project our consciousness to other places, do the same with the physical body, and even to be in two places at once holds enormous potential. So, if you hold any Airline shares, I should sell right now!

And once you see
That all along,
        while you were striving,
                driven
        by the fear
                of future want,
You have been given
What you need –
                riches –
                        bounty,
                Powers galore,
        enough to feed
        the neediest of men,

Then
        can
And always will come
More
        and more to you
From some undreamed-of,
        quite
Unemptiable store.

Chapter Seven

Evolving Towards Humanity

There is evidence there may have been civilisations on Earth far earlier than science can prove. Ancient documents, folk memories, myths, artefacts, buildings like the pyramids, ancient cities in South American jungles, monasteries in remote parts of the Himalayas, all demonstrate technologies that we cannot replicate today. David Hadda's poem places the past in a new perspective:

> The past?
> Erase – and leave no trace
> that might debase
> Your present place in time –
> that timeless space.
> The climber, summit-bound,
> Must be entirely committed
> to the ground under his feet:
> Your base-camp,
> the starting point
> Is now irrelevant, hence obsolete.
> And don't forget:
> The summit that you'll reach
> Is not the end
> to your ascent's eternal climb
> to the Sublime
> with which we all eventually
> Must blend:
>
> Man's seeming separation of The Fall
> cannot for long
> Appear to contradict/oppose
> Life's cosmic Oneness –
> that ever unfolding,
> festive
> Heaven(and earth)ly Choral Song.

Well, our base camp in this journey may well be obsolete. Nevertheless, there are useful perspectives to be gained if we can grasp what may have come before our recorded history. I believe that this knowledge has the potential to blow apart much 'scientific opinion' as to our origins that is held to be true today!

I therefore set out to achieve some understanding as to what really went on in the far distant past, and, as a result of my searches, received input from many different sources. I gather information from dowsing (explained elsewhere), direct telepathic communication, and intuitive sources. When I get started on a specific subject, I always find that articles and books related to my research arrive, experts in the field turn up, and related experiences happen; as if all around me is starting to support me. With this investigation, I started to piece the material together, and a remarkable series of stories began to emerge. This chapter, then, is a compilation, a cohesion, from many sources, which together illustrate how we may have got to where we are today...

ATLANTIS AND DNA

It appears that the humanoid form is a design that has existed for aeons of time, and has been expressed in many different ways over that time.

What do I mean by this? Well, let me take the example of the drawings for a house as a metaphor. The design – its plans, elevations, levels, general layout, rooms, the pitch of the roof, etc. – is, when it is all put together, called its architecture. It progresses from first of all existing as a thought form in the mind and imagination of its architect. The second stage is where it moves into expression, as plans and instructions that others can follow, and build. Finally, the house is built.

At that point, we might say that the original thought has both been expressed (as plans), and is manifest (in the building). It now exists in physical manifestation.

The expression of this design however, may involve different materials. For example, the same design of house might be built from timber, bricks, metal sheets, or even simple mud and wattle. The end effect will be very different depending on the materials used, but it's all the same fundamental architecture, springing from the same original idea.

A similar process has happened with the humanoid form. It, too, started as a thought form, a creation which was initially an idea from the Godhead. It was then built, expressed and manifested, at different times over aeons, using the best possible material that was available at the time. Only in this case, the building material was different forms of DNA!

The same human or rather 'humanoid' architecture has been expressed using the best available DNA at different times in pre-history, which are also different stages in the development of the physical planes of existence. Thus, for example, there are humanoid beings who exist at different vibratory levels or frequencies, which, being largely out of sync with our own, are not today a part of our general consciousness. But if we were able to compare, we would see that they all look broadly like us, i.e. with a torso, two arms, two legs, and an intelligent head, in the same general layout as we are used to amongst races on Earth. Since humanity has been in the phenomenon of The Fall (explained in Chapter Four) – moving down through the vibration frequencies, as a means of creating a time structure – these beings, our space brothers and sisters, have become increasingly remote from us.

On planet Earth, it appears that there have been at

least three great forms of DNA which have been the material utilised to express the humanoid design or architecture. The first of these was the very highest form of Reptilian DNA, many millions of years ago. We know that prior to the long domination of the planet by the Dinosaurs, the reptiles represented the major DNA building block on the planet, and many different reptilian forms resulted, including, I believe, one of the earliest humanoid civilisations.

Much later on, the Dinosaurs came into being and were based on a distinctly more sophisticated DNA. They were even more prolific, being the dominant DNA on Earth for around 165 million years. Over this time, they developed to be truly warm-blooded, thus operating effectively in a far wider variety of ambient temperatures than their reptilian forbears.

A documentary recently shown on Satellite TV's Discovery Channel followed an interesting detective story, as several eminent professors in the field of palaeontology, explored ancient sites where dinosaur footprints and tracks, sometimes by the thousand, are to be found. It became evident that there were no tail prints. This may not seem so important, but it makes a dramatic difference to our understanding of dinosaurs. All our pictures of dinosaurs, developed against images first proposed over a hundred years ago, show large tails dragged lizard-like over the ground, and these were all shown to be incorrect. The facts drawn by the research team from imprints left on the ground appear to indicate that, contrary to received wisdom, these tails were balancing devices, and as such, were held out horizontally and clear of the ground leaving no trail.

Over a vast period of time, the documentary illustrated, one major branch of dinosaurs became increasingly upright. The terrifying killing machine called Tyrannosaurus Rex is a good example, as its massive muscular front limbs were far too small to be useful as legs. They had, in fact, evolved to become what we would see as arms: *indeed, a frontal picture of T-Rex shows arms and shoulders that look distinctly human!* To me, they looked not unlike some of the physically overdeveloped competitors in the wrestling matches shown on TV! T-Rex had undoubtedly evolved so that he moved exclusively on two legs.

One professor demonstrated his conclusion of the logical pinnacle of the development of this particular group of dinosaurs, in the form of a full scale model. *His model was of a giant humanoid!* And what do we find in our ancient mythologies? Stories of giants!

Thus, perhaps science is only just beginning to support what the kids' comic strip writers have known for decades: that there were humanoids that developed in the past, based on the same human architecture as our own, and making the highest use of the best DNA that was available when this happened. As an example that avid TV watchers will understand, observe the cold-hearted Cardassians from the popular Star Trek series, who may be said to represent the *Reptoids*; humanoid beings based on and built using the Reptilian DNA. In the same series, the Klingons, altogether warmer beings but very warlike, arguably represent the humanoids based on the Dinosaur DNA, or to use the correct collective term, the *Dinoids.* It seems that the idea of humanoid beings based on different DNA is now tentatively supported by the latest palaeontological findings.

So how does this apply to Atlantis? Well, we are all vaguely aware that complete civilisations have been here before our recorded, or even speculated, history. Indeed they certainly were! First came the Reptoids, humanoid in overall design, but with a distinctly unfeeling, unemotional demeanour; then, perhaps 170 million years later, came Dinoids who being warm-blooded, were in some respects far more like us. Both evolved, ascended to higher frequencies and in turn, left the planet. Both types were highly evolved, by the time they left Earth. In these higher forms they came back to Earth many, many times. I sense, and indeed many channelled sources tell us, that there were (and are) a variety of Reptoid races in the cosmos and there were (and are) a variety of Dinoid races.

This realisation implies something else, something equally dramatic. Not only are there many humanoid races spread all over the farthest reaches of this universe, but since they all appear to have originally evolved here at different times, and subsequently left, planet Earth appears to be the original home-world for all the humanoid races. No wonder they and their UFO spacecraft appear to pay us so much attention!

Indeed not only were there many civilisations spread around the Universe and based on one or other of these two DNA types, but there were almost certainly other DNA derivatives of the humanoid design as well. The comic strips illustrate the possibility of life based on both crustacean DNA and arachnid DNA. Perhaps these too represent some distant memory? *Spider-man liveth?*

A recently published book, *TWO-THIRDS* by David P. Myers and David S. Percy (published by Auliff), records in story form, how the Alteans (who I believe were an advanced Dinoid race) journeyed towards Earth, travelling across galaxies, in order to settle on Mars. There they spent 200,000 years developing a variation based on their own DNA to create the new and enhanced form from which the human being, the third great genetic experiment on Earth, was to be created. According to the book, humans are based on the highest form of DNA found in our native, warm-blooded species, the anthropoids, whose genetic structure had been cross-engineered by the Alteans so that many additional and advanced, but mostly still latent, faculties were built in. In just two generations they genetically engineered the native anthropoids of Earth to create the first true humans. This, then, is the missing link that followers of Darwin's theories of natural selection have always looked for in the ascent of man. It's called 'genetic engineering'!

The Alteans observed, managed, and led humans through aeons over their long developmental period. Through all that time, Dinoids remained far more developed humanoids than the humans, since they had existed for immeasurably longer. However, the Dinoid faculties were less capable than those embedded in the human DNA. Their ultimate development could not go as far as was *potentially* available to the human being. So they looked for ways to get around their restrictions in order to develop greater powers.

In particular, Dinoids developed a two-layer soul structure. It appears that they were deeply spiritual beings, with complex spiritual technologies that gave them the facilities to do this, although it was no trivial task, and took aeons to complete. The first layer soul-energy was quite similar to our own. The second layer was a sort of soul-mantle overlaying the first, and holding many extraordinary faculties which we are only just becoming cognisant of today. In essence, this additional energy field provided an extension to their faculties, and meant that they could manifest in and out of the physical plane, using this ability to travel across both time and different dimensions, to teleport and bi-locate as well as to communicate telepathically.

It is important to note the similarity of names between the Alteans (the Dinoid travellers who came back to seed the human experiment here) and the Atlanteans (who, I believe, were ruled by members of this same Dinoid race, but very much later in time).

Although Earth had long since ceased to be the home for a Dinoid civilisation, it seems that they often came here from time to time as leaders, first of Atlantis, and later as the Pharaohs of Ancient Egypt. These beings were exceptionally long-lived, compared with their human charges.

Atlantis existed at a markedly higher frequency than our Earth civilisation today; around three times higher than our own. This means that if an Atlantean at his correct frequency were to stand in front of us today, we would probably not even be able to see him.

The story set out above naturally led me to ask questions on the subject during channelling. The following are extracts from a Quazar discussion on the Dinoids:

There was a time when the evolution of the species on Earth led to a creature (mankind was not here then) a humanoid of the dinosaur lineage. These beings came and multiplied in consciousness and created a whole body of conscious entities. When the end came, as it did, for these earthly Dinoid entities, they could all leave their bodies behind and move to another dimension at will.

You can create on this earth new life-forms. When those life-forms develop, they develop consciousness and that consciousness, as it comes into three-dimensional form, takes more advanced and complex forms than we can explain to you. It really is most incredible what is possible on this planet. When the end came for these Dinoids, they ceased to be in three-dimensional form and created a huge body of consciousness that was able to move on through the universe.

The Dinoids were the most advanced race of humanoids to exist on this planet before the coming of hu-mans as they will evolve now. And yes, you have most accurately defined the other humanoid race, the Reptoids, who evolved most rapidly before the Dinoids. Both had a well-advanced form of communication, though you would not have recognised it! But then, your language is a most limited form of communication. Other species also have trouble understanding that you have a formal sense of communication. Other Reptoid and Dinoid races, descended from those that left Earth for other dimensions so long ago, still exist in the physical in other parts of the universe. They have taken slightly different humanoid form than that which they incarnated on this planet, and they occupy many different planets across the galaxy.

In order to maintain themselves at the higher frequency they required, the Dinoids needed an additional source of energy. The whole civilisation was absolutely dependant for much of what it could do on a marvellous structure known as the Earth energy grid. This grid of energy lines covers the whole of the Earth, and although little of it remained after the fall of Atlantis, it can still be measured today. Indeed the grid itself might almost be called Atlantis, it was such an integral part of Atlantean development and capability, both spiritual and scientific. It would not be far-fetched to say that Atlantis was *both* the Atlantean civilisation and the great and vibrant energy grid on which it was based.

So, how did this grid work? Well, it consisted of a whole system of inter-locking energy structures that between them distribute the twelve great rays – the energy sources which are the building blocks of the Universe – onto the physical planet. These rays provided all that was needed to sustain a most abundant and long life for all physical life forms. Dinoids and hu-mans alike drew on the grid, which was highly energised, for both sustenance (food as we know it today was for pleasure, not survival) and to maintain themselves at this higher frequency. The energy grid also interacted with and energised the soul mantles containing the DNA extension of the ruling Dinoids, giving them greatly enhanced powers. Hu-mans enjoyed this high energy of the grid, but, for them, there was a crucial difference in its importance, they were actually capable of living without it. For the Dinoids, however, it was essential for their survival. Eventually, this difference was to become a source of great discontent, and for many, danger.

The reason for this was that all the remarkable powers that the Dinoids had by virtue of engineering their energy-based oversoul, were built into the Human DNA as standard; engineered in earlier times by that very same Dinoid race, the Alteans. The ruling Dinoids were fully aware that at some future time, these hu-mans who they ruled over would become more powerful than them. Indeed throughout the Universe there had been great disquiet expressed about the human experiment. Never had so many powers been packaged into one DNA form. To these powers was added the concept of complete free will and self-determination, and this combination of power and freedom seemed foolish in the extreme to many beings. Consequently, the great human experiment caused a split at every level of sentient life across our Universe. Groups that are recorded in the Bible such as the

Elohim (said to be the creator gods responsible for the physical construction of the universe – a sort of sub-contract team to God!), the Melchezedek Order (a cosmic priesthood), the Essenes (who were cosmic guides to various humanoid groups, and who, on Earth, were responsible for the spiritual training of the young Jesus), the Angelic realms, all these cosmic groupings and others, were deeply split over this plan. It was truly the most fundamental source of the separation that was to follow, and was eventually to affect every level of our Universe.

This same argument surfaced in Atlantis in several ways. First, there was much genetic engineering performed on the humans, in particular by certain visiting Pleiadean races who were reptilian in nature. The modifications were designed to slow down the human development. The Dinoids too performed experiments, trying to graft the human DNA into themselves to gain the benefits of the greatly enhanced DNA.

There have been many theories as to the probable cause of the downfall of Atlantis. Perhaps each of these theories has some truth to it, as several downward trends appeared over the same time-frame. Ultimately, however, the downfall of Atlantis was at least partly to do with the misuse of the great energy grid which was its key support tool, and kept Atlantis at a constant, high vibratory level.

A very powerful Atlantean faction were diverting grid energy to fashion great experiments in advanced energy structures. They did not fully comprehend what they were doing and misuse, or use without full understanding led to abuse. In the wrong hands these devices could be operated as very powerful weapons of war, which could, through the use of massive crystal accumulators, deliver a blast of energy with an effect not unlike a modern nuclear weapon.

It was inevitable that, eventually, they were used in this way. Indeed, most of our deserts today are said to result from this devastating experimentation and later military action. At the same time the use of these powerful weapons caused many of the Earth's tectonic plates to rupture, which gave rise to huge volcanic activity. Eventually, in conjunction with many other factors, this caused a dramatic movement of the main plate on which Atlantis stood.

Before this happened and before the use of these systems for military purposes escalated, the great energy beings of the Cosmos, in whose gift the continuing supply of energy for the grid lay, became increasingly disapproving of the misuse of that gift. At the same time the Dinoid rulers became more and more arrogant about their powers. The fact is that the Dinoids were acting increasingly like Gods to the human population, and they liked being Gods! The energy beings could see the great structural damage being done to the planet, and sent many concerned messages to this effect; the Atlantean rulers simply would not listen, or were no longer inclined to hear.

In the Cosmos, it was eventually decided that the energy must be disconnected, and the grid supply almost completely discontinued, and that planet Earth would consequently go into 'The Fall' as the Bible calls it. *The lack of energy support meant that the planet and all beings on her would now fall steadily down through the energy frequencies.*

During the time of Atlantis and a fully energised grid, the crossover points of the major lines of the grid gave rise to huge energy vortices. The hu-mans of Atlantis, in particular, were told never to spend time in or near these points, as they would quickly become energetically overcharged, which could, in extremes, be fatal. The vortices were so powerful that at times, the energy could clearly be seen rather like a minor Aurora Borealis, with moving 'fingers' of energy, many tens of feet high, pointing upward from the vortex. These vortex points also had some intelligence, so that they could protect themselves in the energetic sense; a daunting prospect to anyone foolish enough to intrude! To the less developed hu-mans this intelligent energy body looked like the mouth of a dragon and gave rise to leylines being referred to as 'dragon lines' in many parts of the world, even today.

Once the decision to cut off the gift of the cosmic energies was made, in order for the grid itself to be de-commissioned, it was necessary for the vortices to be switched off. A small, highly spiritual group of Atlanteans had always opposed the science of the energy experiments, and the resulting war machine that was developed by the diverting of the energy grid. This group was asked to assist by the cosmic energy beings. Their task was to walk into the main vortex points at great personal danger and to use their spiritual powers to switch off the vortex. Small teams were sent all over the planet so that all the vortices could be disabled in this way. This gave rise to mythological stories like St. George and the Dragon; my sense is that he was in fact one of these Atlanteans who remained true to their ideals and their great spirituality and accepted this difficult task. Memories of this 'dragon slaying' era still exist as folk tales in many cultures!

When all the energy points were disabled, what was left was a greatly reduced source and distribution of energy, which consisted of only seven of the great rays, and this at low energy and in a modified and degraded form, which ever since have been reflected in the seven main chakras, or energy centres, of the human body. This was deemed by the cosmic beings to be the minimum energy that could support sentient life.

The decommissioning of the grid was like withdrawing the fixing points that held the grid to the planet. The energy grid literally detached itself from the planet and went off on its own orbit, an 'almost planet' containing all the higher dimensions of earth but not the physical. It left in place only a pale shadow of its former self, causing the start of the fall down through the frequencies, so that the planet would eventually exist at a far lower frequency than previously – lower indeed, than any other physically occupied planet. Thus, Earth was left as a strictly three-dimensional planet, with little of the higher dimensionality that most other planets contain.

Ever since this event, the detached energy grid has come back into conjunction with the Earth every 2,000 years, at which time many apparently magical things have happened for a few years, as the higher powers were temporarily reconnected. The last time this happened was when Christ was on the earth. The grid in the form of a complete planetary energy matrix was known as Herculobus and its energy as Wormwood, this latter being mentioned in the Bible. Only a faint magnetic shadow of the grid, barely detectable, was left on the planet – until recently...

And what of the Dinoids? Without the grid energy to sustain them, their 'oversoul'; the part of them that contained all the magical and energetic powers that gave them the power to rule, was disabled. In fact, the oversoul became a liability, threatening to drain them of their life-energy.

Most of them fled the planet, to look for other energy environments that would sustain them in full power. A few, mostly those with a high degree of dedication to the human experiment, chose to remain, but with power that was greatly decreased because of the removal of the grid. They knew this power would steadily diminish as the energies of the planet became ever lower. The Pharaohs were one Dinoid ruling group that did this, ruling over Egypt for many generations, but with ever less power to fulfil their function as new generations were born. Their great structures such as the Egyptian Pyramids were, in part, collectors of the cosmic energy that could refresh and maintain their powers, but ultimately this only delayed an inevitable end to their rule. Incidentally, it is only now emerging that there are even more impressive pyramids in other parts of our planet, particularly in the more remote rain forests of South America, and dozens in areas of central China. One of the latter is reported to be 1,000 feet high! Presumably these all had the same energy purpose.

All this happened way in the past: let us now look to the present day, because something dramatic, and closely related, has been happening. Over the twelve months of 1995 a phenomenon has been observed, as the energies of the leyline grid has increased a hundredfold. At first no obvious reason could be found for this phenomenon. Then, we realised that the old part of the grid that remained in the Earth was resonating with the approaching 'Herculobus'; the energy matrix without a planet, coming back into its 2,000-year conjunction.

On approximately December 7th, 1995, the grid did indeed come into conjunction with the planet, and, more important, this time it has locked on to stay! This locking-on has meant that humanity is at last ready to be given its powers...on previous occasions, the grid had been here fleetingly, but in effect, had gone straight on past the planet; we simply were not ready for it. Now, our evolutionary task can be fulfilled. Humans are to form the highest level of the grid, by forming heart-to-heart connections between the planet and each other.

At the end of December, ceremonies were performed around the world to start the process of re-commissioning the grid in its true form, enabling it to build up its energy steadily, to a point where it will be highly energised, stable, and multi-dimensional; as will the planet!

Now, at the very end of the 20th century, the grid that gave rise to and supported Atlantis is back and all twelve cosmic energies are present again. Soon all the energetic structures that the grid represents will be in place and operational.

But now, there is something quite new which has been added – an additional thirteenth energy which is only just appearing around the planet for the first time. This energy holds the whole system together and in a form that is highly resistant to abuse (unlike the old system of seven which it replaces and where the energies are easily polarised). This energy is coming into its own for the first time since it was seeded 2,000 years ago. This is the Christ energy which will envelop the whole planet. I do not claim this in any religious sense: what is happening is that the energy structures around us have evolved dramatically. This new energy is what the being we know as Christ came here to anchor 2,000 years ago, and only now is it flooding into the energy grid of the planet. Large changes in energy structures always precede large changes in the physical world. So, the much discussed Ascension is being driven by these vast energy changes: it is the move back up the energy frequencies to where we once were, in the time when the Dinoids reigned, and 'magic' was the order of the day.

There is however one crucial difference, which is that humanity has been tempered by long experience of the fall, by separation, and all the trauma that has gone with it through many hundreds, if not thousands of incarnations. We are very, very different beings from those that were here at the time of Atlantis. We have evolved through many tough incarnations, and collectively integrated huge amounts of experience. I believe that soon, we will be ready to take and use the powers of Atlantis, but in a greatly modified way, to reflect today's unique situation. The nature of the consciousness being brought about by the arrival of the Christ energy means that these powers will be used for the highest good, in an entirely new format, which will eventually benefit the whole cosmos, and will bring about the full expression of the faculties for so long latent in the Hu-man design. *If we succeed in this full expression of our design, what is then on offer, the opportunity that is at hand, is no less than the leadership position, in the occupation and spiritual redemption of the physical Universe!*

We – myself and my editor Nasreen – were just about to sign off the manuscript of this book, and had been looking at this particular chapter, and the notes about the Wormwood consciousness. 'What a shame,' we agreed 'that we don't have just a little more information on this subject'. Our connections duly obliged. Four hours later, Nasreen received an E-mail from Judy Crookes, an active channel in New Jersey, who has been working with an entity called Jacob. She was about to leave on an out-of-town visit, when Jacob absolutely insisted that she do some channelling. She reluctantly obliged and was given some material – she did not understand the context as she had no idea of the discussion I had that morning with Nasreen – with the accompanying instruction to send it to Nasreen. Judy must have started her work within a very short time after our agreeing we needed more information...!

Here, with comments from me, is what she sent us. Jacob says:

For within the time/space continuum there is an inconsistency in the framework which you have structured here on this planet. You are ready to fix that at this point in your "history".

This inconsistency consists of the involvement of the soul in the plane that you call reality. You see, you have never been able to allow the soul to become involved within your creations on the scale which is possible for the mechanism was not there. It has been, shall we say, with one hand tied behind your backs that you have advanced as far as you have as a human race.

Very interesting! This implies that there is a part of us which is separated from our physical body by some damage to the space-time continuum. To go on:

The hole within the time/space continuum is what I will call a leak. There is a space there wherein the soul cannot participate within your day-to-day activities. This leak is an energy leak and it causes the input of the soul to be disregarded by the average human. It is only with increased strength of mental focus and energy focus that you have been able to reaffirm your attachment to your soul. And to invite its participation in your life patterns.

Now you are ready to fix this leak and to enable the rest of mankind to begin to participate on the same level as those who have been striving for spiritual perfection. This leak is nothing more than a reverse vortex, it is and has been sucking out the energy rather than bringing it in, which it was originally designed to do.

It seems that we are to be given the same status and abilities as the most spiritual amongst us, if the damage to this continuum can be fixed – which is apparently up to us! Even more interesting, I had always thought that the major vortices had been turned off at the end of Atlantis. Here, we are being told that one was actually reversed, and has been 'sucking out' energy ever since. No wonder we went into 'the Fall'!

You see, when you, as a race, developed to the point wherein which you were using your powers of creation in a harmful fashion, when the crystals of Atlantis began to be used as tools of destruction, there was created this reverse vortex to enable the energy that was building up within the planet to escape. This is commonly known in this time as the Wormwood Consciousness. This consciousness that left the planet, it is that which is meant to be used for full connection with the soul.

This seems to be consistent with what we have said to date. Clearly from this text, we cannot as human beings, be fully expressed without it. To continue:

Now, even in the time of Atlantis, this connection did not exist fully, for there was much development that needed to be done. But it acted like a seed energy and was mean to be used as a vehicle for the completion of the act of soul union. Of course, because of the destruction, conscious destruction, this never came about.

So, the Wormwood energy was in the course of development, and its functionality never properly implemented, when the Atlantean crash came. It was important that we did not go through the metamorphosis to a higher form, just as bizarre warring struggles were seemingly engulfing humanity. The solution was this:

The vortex that was used to funnel this powerful energy away from a self-destructing mankind was left in place, so that the energy could be replaced at a later time.

Apparently, we now have the opportunity to put right the draining effect of these reversed vortices. This is what needs to be, and is being, done:

This vortex now needs to be reversed and rewound, so that it can be used to reinsert the energy back into place.

The devices that need to be built have been under construction for some time and some are aware of that which we speak. Those who have been working on the light grid of the planet, are somewhat knowledgeable about this mechanism. Those who have not been working on the grid have been enjoying the fruits of the energy work that others have done. Such is the exchange of energy here that those who are enjoying are beginning to move very quickly into place as light beings of their own capacity.

However, it appears to be those who are just beginning to come into awareness of things spiritual who will add their weight (in the energetic sense) and really get things moving:

These newer beings are the ones who will tip the scale, so to speak, and will make the vortex begin to work towards its inevitable reversal. This concept would blow the minds of the scientist in the world, but it is possible to do this work purely on the mental and emotional plane. This is where the physical is not at all necessary. So, those who are working towards connection with soul are working towards reversing the direction of this vortex. This connection with the soul, once made, will enable the energy that has been removed so long ago (in your terms) to again begin its job on this planet.

One way of determining when soul connection is underway is when an individual develops a caring and responsible attitude towards his environment and fellow human beings; when he has spontaneous spiritual experiences; when he begins to see elementals and ghosts of projections of past times; when he is given strange new powers of healing, clairvoyance, guiding voices or the like; and many other such phenomena. All these point to a raising of the vibratory level and a strengthening connection with the soul part (also called our higher selves, our guardian angels) of who we are. Jacob then reinforced the point about those who are newly awakened to these things, and here explains what the end effect will be:

Do you understand that those who are in the process of connection are the ones who will eventually make the whole reversal possible? This is what will happen, for you see, it will not take too much more energy "push" to cause this to happen. It will take very little to tip the scale in the other direction. And all of mankind will benefit.

What happens when a vortex changes its direction? It has been said that the poles will reverse. No, this is not what will happen, but the poles on the earth will shift. Mankind will no longer be able to claim that they have been to the north or south poles, for they will no longer be in the same position. This sucking of the vortex has been what has caused the shifts that have taken place in the past.

Now, be aware that this change in the poles will not cause the kind of major deconstruction that has taken place in the past. For you see the energy in the planet is not going to create havoc. The energy in the planet is waiting and willing to receive. There is a different vibrational pattern than existed in the past. This is not to say that there will not be some kinds of changes in the planet. For there will be, but they will not be of the totally destructive nature that existed in the past, such as the great flood, which not only inundated the entire planet, but also decreased the population of the earth.

*So, this information is meant to give to those of you who are in the state of wonderment over the connection with their soul to know that the energy to do, to accomplish, is on its way and that you should enable yourself to receive the energy. Just as you create the energy as you go forth on this quest, you will also receive back so much more than you can possibly put into it. This is because you get back **all** that has been put in, not just what you have put in. This is the concept of return. It is not return to you of what you put in, but return to you of what all of like mind have put in.*

This pathway, this attachment, to the world, for that is indeed what it is, it is literally attached to the world — I am speaking of the vortex again here — this attachment is finding that it is in love with the energy of the world and is willing to do world service. Now, one must be aware of the fact that all energy has a choice, all energy has consciousness. It can all make decisions, on whatever level it exists. On whatever level it exits, the decisions that can be made are appropriate to that energy. So the inversion of the vortex is being made with great intelligence. And being made by a being who is fully knowledgeable of the profound effects that it will have upon society as a whole.

The return of this Wormwood energy will thus allow those who seek connection to make that connection and to leave this attachment to this earth plane. There are simultaneous attachments that are in existence, for you see, the soul is not a one plane energy, in some instances. There are those, of course who are "new" to creation and are within this sphere of existence exclusively. There are many, however, who are co-existent within many different planes, may different arenas. Their love affair with the earth plane has enabled the growth of all the other parts of their soul to grow simultaneously."

A stunning message, sent almost as an 'afterthought' to the book by the cosmic beings. It illustrates that something very powerful is happening with the return and completion of the Wormwood energy, that this phenomenon is linked to our consciousness, and that it will lead to our full 'soul connection' and to understanding what it means to become multi-dimensional... and that there is nothing to be frightened about, although I think we may all be in for an 'interesting ride'.

Personally, you can count me in...

IN PERSPECTIVE

If life was here
Uncounted billion years ago,
What do I need to fear
        with my own
                little
                        dotty lot!

Even with our smearing
                the surface of this star,
      our mucking up of its atmosphere,
The earth has dealt so far
      all on its own
            in one way or another:
I guess our caring Mother
Can cope with cleaning up after her messy
                        pups.

      And even
If not – the Universe
Won't go to pot:
Should this one grain of sand
Somewhere on life's galactic ocean-strand
Come to an end,
      all
Will go on
      in its peculiar way –
           for all we know,
Another Bang
      will blow another
        and another
Quite different Creation into being
    that you and I
Will not be seeing.

Chapter Eight

Earth Energies And The DNA Blueprint

Over the years I have come to realise the importance of energy to the physical world, not just the energy we consume, but the fact that every atom around us is ultimately an energy structure. That's what Einstein expressed in his formula:

$$E=mc^2.$$

E is the amount of energy, while M is the mass of the body in question, and c is the speed of light! The formula can also be expressed as $M = E/c^2$ which put into words, is perhaps easier to understand. All it basically means is 'it takes a vast amount of energy to create mass'.

If huge amounts of energy have been drawn together somehow, to create things, it would be logical to think that there might be important energy fields around every physical item around us. And, indeed, around each of us!

Human beings were once far more spiritual in form than we mostly are today. We are so enamoured with the material world, that we have lost a great many valuable spiritual concepts and capabilities – although I believe we are about to make a great leap toward integrating the physical with the spiritual from all our past experiences!

One aspect of this move back to the spiritual awareness of the past is the idea of our subtle bodies. It is believed by many that we have not just one body, but several, each overlaid in the same approximate space. Whereas the body that we can all see is physical, the other bodies are structures of living energy around us, each with a different function. Only people with a special gift or training are normally able to see these energy bodies. It is these bodies that we normally cannot see that are referred to by many healers as our subtle bodies. Perhaps the easiest of our energy structures with which to demonstrate their existence is the heat body. A picture taken with an infra-red camera will show a large red 'bubble' around the body of a person being photographed, and the bubble extends well outside the physical body. If you hold the palm of your hand open towards and a few inches away from another person, you can demonstrate the same heat body a different way; you should be able to feel it!

There are a number of other subtle bodies such as the emotional body, which reaches far beyond the physical body. We often notice that if someone in a room is very angry or distressed, or has any other strong emotion running, then we 'pick up the vibes', and are affected by their condition. This is because their body of emotion 'touches' our body of emotion.

Different spiritual philosophies recognise different subtle bodies, but in addition to the physical body, the most commonly recognised are the emotional body, the mental body, and the spiritual body. A type of camera, using a technique called 'Kirlian photography', can take pictures which demonstrate many of the energies which are outside our normal visual range, but clearly shown in the resulting photographs. These subtle bodies seem to go into other dimensions in some way, and I am sure that their recognition and conscious use will turn out to be the key to enabling many of our latent faculties.

On one occasion, I asked Quazar (who tells us he is a pure energy being) how he 'saw' us. The question was in the context of an enquiry about the technique of using coloured light for healing. Here is his reply:

Colours carry energy which, when associated with Human form can dissolve the knots and other blockages in that form. The human form is, in energetic terms and as seen from my perspective, like a bundle of knotted spaghetti. Colour, like sound, is associated with, has the the power if you will, to untangle parts of the spaghetti.

It seems to me that Quazar, as an energy being sees us only at the energy level. Our physical bodies appear quite transparent to him!

The planet also has its energy bodies, although this knowledge has been lost in antiquity. However, in 1995 we received some channelling that showed that the energy forms around each human being, are actually a microcosm of the energies of our planet.

Peter: Can you tell us what you mean by the human energy grid?

Quazar: The human energy body is merely a hologrammatic replica of the earth.

Peter: So the human being is a microcosm of the earth, in effect?

Quazar: If you will, that is so.

Peter: We hear a great deal about the effect of this on our DNA blueprint, and some of the chemical structures of the body. Can you tell us about this?

Quazar: As we have said, the cellular structure of the human being is being activated by the twelve energies now being focused on earth.

Here, Quazar refers to the twelve 'archetypal' energies of the cosmos which have, in stepped-down form, been newly re-attached and activated on the surface of the planet, and indeed, in human consciousness, by the arrival of the Heculobus body. To continue:

Peter: Can you explain what you mean by 'the cellular structure being activated'?

Quazar: The deepest form, the smallest level of the molecular structure, are receptors of these twelve energies. As the human body receives these energies the cells are re-awoken.

Peter: And the effect of this is...

Quazar: The cellular structure of the human body will be changing, as will the energetic system of the

human body. The energy grid of the human
form will have activated twelve energy centres,
as will the energy grid of the planet.

This refers to the human chakra system, a series of points in the physical body from each of which emanates a vortex of energy. These chakra centres are additional to the subtle energy bodies, and operate in a different frequency range. As the new energies come into the planet, the chakra system appears to be changing from a system of seven main energy centres in the body to a twelve-centre system (there are many smaller energy points as well). Once all twelve energies are in place – this applies to both the planet and the human body – a further phenomenon takes place: what we might call the Christ energy (as discussed in the previous chapter) also begins to be present. This is not a narrow religious concept; it is an energy of transformation, that assists each human to move effectively through the changes that are now taking place. Although there may be other names for this energy, it is starting to be received by people of every race, creed, culture and political persuasion.

For those who understand the conventional chakra system, the new chakra system appears to consist of the following twelve energy centres:

- The base of spine chakra disappears, and the old 'hara' just above the sexual organs becomes the first chakra.
- The Solar Plexus chakra divides into two, one inside the other: dealing with intuition and emotion.
- The heart chakra becomes a 'nested' set of three: the interpersonal heart, the humanity connection, and the cosmic heart connection. The old throat chakra will merge with the interpersonal heart (meaning that, to be at this level, what we believe in our hearts must align with what we say with our mouths! *Very* challenging!).

- A new chakra appears at the mouth, and is sound activated, as a key to other dimensions.
- The third eye remains in place.
- The crown chakra remains in place.
- A new chakra appears inside the crown chakra, function not yet understood. Possibly access to multi-dimensional awareness.
- A new chakra appears at the very top of the head, and is the intake point for cosmic breath, or 'prahna' (something we mostly forgot about long ago!).
- An existing chakra about fifteen inches above the head will become properly activated for the first time. This is the energy trans-dimensioning chakra, giving us constant access to energies from other dimensions and facilitating the whole new chakra system.

It would take a whole book to explain the importance of these energy centres. The salient overview is that each of us is being completely re-structured at the energy level. Our new faculties will be supported by the ability to draw energy constantly from higher dimensions – once we learn how! Quazar continues on this subject:

Peter: *Will this happen to all human beings at the same time or will some be in advance of others?*

Quazar: *It depends how much you allow yourself to receive the energies.*

Peter: *And how far through the process is the planet, and humanity, at the moment?*

Quazar: *Approximately 30 to 50 per cent, depending on where one looks – not all parts are activated at the same rate.*

The point is that the chakra energy centres in the human body exactly reflect similar energy points found on the Earth's surface. These are rapidly being energised in a new form, so that the energetic rise of planet and human are inextricably linked. I got a glimpse of this when I got involved in an adventure that started in October 1993.

THE GLASTONBURY VORTEX

I have always been fascinated by UFOs and have indulged in much of speculation about what they run on; the source of their motive power! A few years ago I was told that certain types of electrostatic engines – devices that create very high voltage static charges, which in turn generate a vacuum – were used to power one of the commonest designs of UFO. Although I was unsure what to think of the many UFO stories that were emerging at that time, I was given an article to read which dealt knowledgeably with this technology, and I was very interested in it, and intrigued about the many possibilities this could open up.

In essence the article stated that if a very large static charge was created on one surface of a ship, a vacuum would be constantly created, and the ship drawn forward into it, thus creating rapid forward motion. My curiosity in this theory was fuelled by the fact that it might have application to the Airship project which I was involved with, as I have described in another story in this book. I decided to ascertain if there was a scientific basis for this theory and asked a Professor friend who was extremely knowledgeable in this area, if the technology I had learned about might, at least, be theoretically possible. He felt that there were some precedents that at least went part of the way towards this concept – machines in which an 'electronic wind' could be created by electromagnetism. Encouraged by this, I decided to try and gain confirmation of this viewpoint and see if our channelling might help us by revealing additional or supplementary material.

So, in 1993 while doing some channelling work, I asked to speak to a being called Adama. We had been introduced to this entity some months previously, when he had been channelled by our friends Shield and Sharula. At that time, he had demonstrated that he had great knowledge of the different classes of UFOs and their technologies, and more importantly, he was able to communicate this to us in terms we could understand and relate to.

We started our channelling session in the usual manner according to a well-established protocol, and asked for Adama. Moments later, Adama came through, and I addressed him on the question of how much information was available about various UFO drive technologies. Somewhat mystifyingly, all he would say to us was "Go to Glastonbury!", which sentence was repeated in response to each of three different questions I asked him – although, to his last response he added, "you will be surprised who you might meet over breakfast!".

This seemed a very strange answer, but Adama had repeated the essence of his message three times and we had learned to take these things seriously. Besides, we could never resist the promise of an adventure, so I agreed with Oonagh that at the first opportunity, we would indeed go to Glastonbury.

The town of Glastonbury and its surroundings in the county of Somerset in England, has a reputation as a 'New Age' centre. There is much to see. There are the ruins of the massive Abbey which was destroyed in the Reformation. The Chalice Well is another great attraction, and then there is the Tor, a strange hill, looking as if it were crafted by some long-lost civilisation, with a Church Spire at the top. Its shape acts powerfully upon the psyche, and there are many legends associated with it. The most popular one states that King Arthur disappeared into the Tor, to return at some future time when his country needs him!

The Tor forms a kind of energetic knot; the point in which two major Leylines (Earth energy lines) cross. One of them – the Michael line – goes from the Wash (half way up the east coast of England) all the way down to St Michael's Mount in Cornwall (the south west corner of the country), while the other one, the Mary line, passes down through the Pennines (north-south, roughly down the middle of England) to the middle of the south coast. At the Tor, they inter-twine up the spiral pathway leading up to the top, and cross at the very apex of this strange landmark! All in all, there is much to investigate in this ancient town; enough to keep one happy for hours!

Some weeks after the Adama channelling, Oonagh took two days off from her work, so that we could make a long weekend of it, and off we went. We were playing it by ear; we had no hotel booking, and little idea as to what we were there to do. Since there were no agendas we started by doing what any good tourist might, and went to look at Glastonbury Abbey as our first stop. We explored the ruins, felt the energies, and, in the gathering gloom of a late November afternoon, saw all that we could in the time available.

As we left the Abbey grounds, I spotted a very interesting crystal shop – The Crystal Cave. We went in for a browse, when I saw a notice on the wall, announcing 'First Class Bed and Breakfast Available: ask at the counter'. We had made no arrangement as to where we might stay. It was getting quite dark, and this seemed a distinct possibility, so we asked. Half an hour later, we were knocking at the door of

Shamballah, a Spa and Healing Centre on the lower slopes of Glastonbury Tor.

A large, blond lady, called Mary Tara, greeted us as we entered, arms akimbo, demanding, "Well, where have you been? I have been waiting for you". As we had never seen her before, this came as something of a surprise, but very shortly we were communicating with each other like long-lost friends.

This was the start of a quite different adventure! We had planned to stay overnight, but ended up at Shamballah for three days. On the first morning Mary Tara asked if I would try some meditation with her. Now, I have been taught to meditate, but cannot say I practise it with great dedication! However, something was definitely 'in the air', so I readily agreed. We went to a secluded room, sat down facing each other, and began...Mary Tara said she was seeking information. She would not say what it was, or how I was involved, but asked if I would explore a visualisation through meditation, and she would give me some guidelines. I did not think much would happen, but kept an open mind and said I was willing to try.

After I spent some minutes with my eyes closed, getting 'attuned to the energies', Mary Tara asked me to visualise myself going below the ground outside the house. An unusual request, but I focused myself on this task, and was surprised when a few moments later, I not only saw the ground outside in my imagination, but it opened up, allowing me to go down below its surface. I had the strangest sensation of descending through billowing clouds, strongly tinged with purple. As I continued downwards, I became aware of a light, somewhere far below me, and glowing warmly through many cloud layers. As my descent continued, all the while the light was getting brighter.

While I was having this rather un-worldly experience, I was simultaneously giving a spoken commentary to Mary Tara, who muttered a few quiet words of encouragement as I went on with my journey. Down, down, with the light below me getting ever brighter...Eventually, something started to emerge from the billowing clouds, and I saw a great, multi-faceted crystal, many feet high. It was filled with light, but nevertheless, it was very sickly to look at. The light seemed to be 'bleeding' away from its base, and it looked downright, well, *anaemic* (if that is an appropriate term to use about a ten-foot high crystal!).

After I had described every detail of what I 'saw' to Mary Tara, she said to me "Now go back in time, to another place which you will know, and tell me what you see." I followed her instructions, instinctively focusing my thoughts anew, and in a few moments, experienced standing in some kind of temple. Again, I duly reported what I saw. Mary Tara's response was to ask me "Who is standing on either side of you?"

I re-focused on my vision and sensed two people alongside me, one at either shoulder. The energies associated with them seemed very familiar. I concentrated for a few moments longer and it came to me. Yes, the one on my left was definitely Oonagh, my present-day partner who had accompanied me to Glastonbury. The one by my right shoulder was Rajan, an Indian healer and teacher who was also a good friend. He often worked with us when Oonagh and I channelled. We had worked together as a 'triad' – a very powerful energetic formation – for many months now. I identified my companions to Mary Tara who asked, "And who is standing opposite you?"

Again, there was a few moments' pause while I concentrated my inner vision. Again I sensed....there were three people facing us. The one in the middle had piercing yellow-green eyes – exactly like those of Mary Tara! I described the other two people to her, but I felt that I did not know them; at least not yet, in this life!

We ended the meditation at this point, and I slowly came back into the present moment but continued to feel quite spaced out for a while as a result of my experience. Oonagh had joined us, and the three of us then discussed what I had seen. Mary Tara offered us the following explanation:

"All the people you just saw, we all worked together as a small team at the time of the downfall of Atlantis," she told me directly, with total conviction. As detailed in the last chapter, I was already aware of the story of the energy grid and how it had been discontinued after the Atlanteans abused its power in uncontrolled energy experiments, which in turn became weapons of war. "A small group of those who followed the Rule of One," she told me, "came together to be given instructions to assist in the de-commissioning of the Earth grid. They were sent on missions all over the world, to enter the major vortices, and use their spiritual power to switch them off."

I also knew that the Rule of One had been the guiding spiritual philosophy at that time, a belief in only one supreme God. This separated the followers of the Rule of One, those who remained true to centuries of spiritual understanding and commitment, from the other very powerful and influential group of Atlanteans, known as The Sons of Belial, who were into extreme materialism, great self-indulgence and self-aggrandisement.

This 'great divide' of belief existing in Atlantis and the actions of the followers of the Rule of One in de-commissioning the energy grid in order to prevent its further abuse and indeed the destruction of the entire planet, gave rise to a whole body of mythological stories. It arose out of the ancient folk memories of these people who were spiritual warriors, rather than Knights on horseback. This group of people struggled with what the Chinese even today, call the Dragon Lines, while they tried, sometimes at great personal risk, to switch off the energies as they had been asked to do as part of their spiritual task.

Mary Tara then disclosed that in a much earlier lifetime – indeed towards the end of the Atlantean debacle – a group of six of those Atlanteans who followed the Rule of One, the ones I had seen in my vision, had been together at the time when the vortices were shut down. We had been sent out, along with many other similar groups, to do this work. One of our group tasks, those many centuries ago, had been the de-commissioning of the vortex at Glastonbury!

Mary Tara revealed that some months earlier she had been given the information that these very same six people would come together early in January. It was now emerging that the main purpose of this reunion was to begin the long process of re-energising and re-connecting the Glastonbury vortex, and Oonagh, Rajan and I were a part of this group! Mary Tara seemed to know who the other two members of the group were, so Oonagh and I agreed to come back in January, bringing our colleague, Rajan, with us.

On the appointed day, our little group drove down to Glastonbury, and went expectantly to the Healing Centre. In the courtyard at Shamballah there is a huge crystal star, seven-pointed, and about seven feet in diameter. We had previously agreed that this was to be the central point of our ceremony. We were waiting in an adjoining room at the Centre for the others when an elderly man entered the room. I looked at him and involuntarily exclaimed "Merlin!" much to my great surprise. I immediately wondered why, as I was introduced to Major Gordon Smith, a leading practitioner in Radionics, who keeps a stud farm a few miles away just outside the town of Wincanton. I really don't know where my impulsive greeting to him came from, or why, but ever since then the Major has been known to us as Merlin. A little later, Sue, a local healer joined Oonagh, Mary Tara, Rajan, the Major and myself and our little group was complete.

We stood around the star, powerful invocations were made, and a great deal of mystical work was accomplished. Gradually the energies of the great crystal beneath the Tor were re-awakened to the best of our ability. It was a highly effective ceremony which stirred up a great deal of energy. At one point, great gusts of wind materialised and circled around the crystal star in a huge vortex of energy, and for a few moments we found it difficult to stay on our feet. It seemed to me that the energetic work that we were doing had evoked a very strong response from the natural world. We ended the ceremony once we felt that the re-connection was made, and gratefully – since it was a cold January day – trooped into the kitchen for steaming hot mugs of tea. We all agreed that since this was only the beginnings of the process, we would meet again, over the crystal star in two weeks time to further the process which we had started.

In fact, we went back twice, each time reinforcing the energetic work we had done on that cold January day. It seemed to be working, and it had been a great adventure. I had certainly learned a great deal that was new and had been given much to think about... However, we had become so engaged in this whole adventure, I must admit that I had completely forgotten the original reason for going to Glastonbury in the first place, over three months earlier!

At the end of the last visit, we packed up our belongings (we had stayed overnight and went into the town centre to say 'goodbye' to Mary Tara, who was working that morning at The Crystal Cave. We were just about to leave when she said, "Oh, by the way, there is someone I want you to meet", and led me to a corner of the shop where a man in his thirties was browsing. I was distinctly reluctant to do this, as I had mentally set myself a schedule for the day and was anxious and impatient to get on the road. Nevertheless, I told myself, it would not hurt to spend a few moments saying 'hello' to this person.

We started talking and my new acquaintance soon told me that he had been channelling entire blueprints of technologies some of which were completely alien to him and remained a mystery. He had, however, become so dedicated to his work on this material, that he had sold up his house and the shop that he had been running, and started to build several of these devices with the proceeds. I asked him to describe one of these machines he was working on.

You can imagine my surprise and indeed, astonishment, when he started to describe something that he thought might be some sort of drive or engine, and I immediately recognised key elements of the electrostatic drive system I had asked Adama about, all those months before!

We had come full circle!

The living
Are my main concern;
    the out of life
Must wait their turn,
    though they be
All-enfolding essence
       to my present form –
In form my structure,
          functions
Within the detailed space,
The hour allots
To you and me.

But still,
The day
Has right of way
As will the other plane
When the terrestial traffic-lights
Concede to it
Priority.

Chapter Nine

Cosmic Energies And Archetypes

Although I understood that a huge energy body had approached, and attached itself to the planet (see Chapter 7) and this was part of the natural order of things, I felt that I needed to understand how these energies were distributed around the planet, and try to pull the whole story together. My knowledge of this aspect began early in 1995, nearly a year before the arrival of the energy body. It all started with a half-hour visit to a car boot sale...

THE TWENTY PENCE ADVENTURE

Quite often, I have found myself in an adventure which has built up over a period of time, gradually revealing itself as information has come in from many different directions which in turn started to indicate a larger picture, leading to a compelling story when all the pieces of the jigsaw have been assembled. This story was one which unfolded in just this kind of way.

I have always been aware that I have a strong connection with Hermes, the being deified by the ancient Greeks, though he appears to have been a factor in our planetary history since long before that. It transpires, from my looking up this deity in an Encyclopaedia of Mythology, that Hermes was able to go to 'heaven or hell, and his energy was sufficiently robust that he would not be touched by either'. This however is not his most dominant aspect. Hermes was most noted as a geomancer; that is to say, he was the being who originally set up the energy grid and hence the structure on which the physical planet Earth is built. Strange, then, that I have never had any interest in Geomancy, or so I thought! Then one day, it all started to change...

The local school is a five minutes' walk from the houseboat in which I live. Once every month, on the first Sunday morning, the school holds a 'car boot sale' in its grounds. Being an inveterate browser I found it very interesting, with many stalls displaying everything from complete junk to useful handyman tools, second-hand gadgets, and the occasional 'find'. Indeed, I have regularly found small pieces of silver, antique cut-glass items, and other ageing goodies!

On this particular occasion, I strolled down to the school on a bright, early spring Sunday morning in 1995, and spent a good half-hour rooting around amongst the many stalls, looking for things of interest. As usual I resolved not to spend more than 20 pence on any single item. This ensured that any purchase I took a fancy to was likely to be good value! I walked up to a stall which caught my attention, by virtue of the fact that it had a particularly interesting range of items, and the stallholder had also taken the time and trouble to display these to advantage.

I commented on this while browsing through his stock. "Congratulations, on a really well-stocked stall. You should do well today!"

"Yes," he said. Then, by way of passing the time, he added pleasantly, "I can see how I might sell almost everything here – except for these! I don't even know what they are supposed to do!" He pointed out a strange pair of 'L'-shaped rods, with collars on the shorter part of the 'L'.

Something about them instinctively took my fancy. "Well," said I impulsively, "How much do you want for them then?"

"20 pence and they are yours," came the response.

After a few moments of fumbling for change, I became the proud owner of an excellent and very sensitive pair of dowsing rods; the basic tools of the leyline hunter, leylines being an aspect of geomancy!

I must explain that leylines constitute a grid of energy lines that criss-cross the country and cover the entire planet. There are many books on the subject, ranging from the popular to the deeply academic. The original re-discovery was made early in this century by The Reverend Alfred Watkins, who after much research wrote a book called *The Old Straight Track* which documented his many findings, since when the subject has become widely accepted and researched. From reading some of these books, it seems that the ancient tribes who inhabited the earth always knew that these lines were there, and used them in many ways. So did the builders of churches, and other religious buildings, who right up to the end of the last century, always constructed their places of worship on conjunctions of leylines, where the energy is greatest.

In present-day England, one of the easiest ways to find the energy lines on a map is to join up all the old Church sites. You will be astounded how many of them are placed on the same line, all the way across the country.

In the case of the two best-known lines – the Michael line, which passes from the Wash on the east coast to the coast of Cornwall in the south west, and the Mary line, which passes down from the Pennine Hills, there are even many villages and churches which include the names Michael or Mary!

Until recently, the energies in these lines have been very subtle, and only a very sensitive technique, and a pair of dowsing rods, could find them at all. But it seems that some people just have a natural affinity with finding and plotting them; the knack, as it were.

I was given a brief demonstration of how to use the dowsing rods, by Richard, a friend who had long experience of using dowsing rods. I immediately got to work with them and found that I had a skill that was very sensitive, and I could find the leylines quickly and easily. Even more interestingly, I appeared to be given large amounts of additional information about each line or conjunction site. The delivery of this material was somewhere between telepathic and intuitive, and appeared to be coming from elsewhere i.e. not in my conscious self, whenever I did dowsing work. I also discovered very quickly that the results of my dowsing were starting to tie up with another area of study that I had been working on for many months. This was getting to be quite fascinating!

This study is based on the fact that at one level, everything around us is made of energy. Atomic scientists have long since known this. Einstein's ubiquitous formula ($E = mc^2$) merely states that it takes a huge amount of energy to make matter. Our atomic and hydrogen bombs demonstrate this dramatically, as the great explosions they cause is the energy from de-materialising just a few ounces of nuclear material! It seemed to me that there must be many forms of energy required to create material existence, and that there might be a way of 'codifying' energy.

For some time my mind had been exercised by the question, 'What are the energy building blocks around us, and what is their nature?' and the answer to that question. It seemed more than likely that there were many types of energy that made up the solid matter of which our world is created.

I read many books and articles on the subject, and slowly began to realise that these building blocks did indeed exist. There were twelve 'master' energies that constitute the building blocks of the universe. These are also known as the 'Twelve Great Rays'. In addition to these 'pure' energy types, there appear to be many,

many combinations of these energies which form complex interference and interactive patterns that assist in creating the physical world.

Furthermore, it seems now that if all twelve Rays are present in any one place, then a thirteenth Ray appears, which in some way completes the set and holds the whole system of energies together. Later in my studies, I was to learn that this thirteenth ray is what many people would call the Christ energy; the third part of what the bible refers to as 'The Trinity'.

The actual master Rays exist at very high frequency, way beyond that which we experience with our sensory faculties of sight, sound and smell. What is important is the relationship between these energies. There appear to be fixed ratios between any two rays, in terms of their individual frequencies. These very high frequency Rays are then stepped down many times, through a huge spectrum of frequencies, but always maintaining the ratios between each other, until they come into the frequency range that we physically experience as light, sound and vibration.

The musical scale is a very good illustration of 'Ray' energies. If you play any chromatic musical scale from the middle of the piano keyboard with the semitones, there áre twelve plus one in an octave, the last being the octave itself. There are other octaves above and below the one you just played, which contain the same notes, but at higher or lower pitch or frequency. This both illustrates the concept of how the great Rays are stepped down through frequency, and also represents them, since the musical octave along with its semitones is a good replication of the frequency ratios.

I learned that these Rays at their highest level, are known to have intelligence, and specific characteristics as they affect human beings, and I started tabulating these characteristics. This information came to me over the next year period from the end of 1994, before I acquired my dowsing rods, through another odd story.

We were on our way to celebrate the New Year at Hazelwood House, a big old Victorian guest house and retreat in South Devon, where our friends there were hosting perhaps forty guests. It was a three-hour drive, and on the way we decided to do a little work on the energies and techniques we knew about to date. We discussed the subject as I drove, and Oonagh noted a list of items in her diary. Our main focus was on the techniques of manifesting, and on the energy systems. Over the New Year we had a great time (as always at Hazelwood) and returned home two days later.

On our way back, we decided to call in on Victor and Donna, two good friends of ours. We spent a happy afternoon, and just before we left, Donna said, "Oh, by the way, I looked out a book for you." She handed me a small white book, called *The Seven Mighty Elohim*. Published in the early 1950s, it had detailed information on each of the Rays, and the beings, the Elohim, who ultimately controlled them. I was even more astonished when we discovered that the seventh Ray was controlled by Arcturus, the being that we had been in channelled contact with for almost two years! Of course, we still had to learn about the other six Rays, but this was a great start.

A few months after that, I started to look for leylines with my newly acquired dowsing rods, and my intuition began telling me something: the energy in the lines varied from line to line in some way. At this point I decided to use a different kind of dowsing, by swinging a crystal on a fine chain, over a chart which was designed to give a certain range of answers. This was something I had done many times before. I now asked a range of questions around these leyline energies.

First, I asked, 'How many types of energy, differentiated by frequency, are to be found in these lines?' The answer I was given was 12! Hmmm...food for thought!

I wondered if these might be the same as the universal energy building blocks I had been studying. I used the crystal, over a percentage chart (showing 0 – 100 percent) and asked 'To what extent, expressed as a percentage, is there a relationship between these leyline energies, and the twelve great Rays?' Perhaps the answer – 100% – should not have been a surprise, but never the less, it was! By this time I was definitely excited. It seemed that the energies in these very faint leylines exactly and precisely reflected the energy building blocks of the universe.

So, it was becoming apparent that the energy grid that was known to cover the Earth, might well be energised by drawing in the cosmic energies that are the building blocks of the universe! Powerful stuff!

I devised some more questions. I made up a chart with twelve sectors, in which I noted each of the twelve rays, by number. I allowed for a thirteenth, by indicating a circular motion if this energy should be present. For each leyline I had identified, I then went back and asked 'Which energy is running in this leyline?' and it immediately became clear that they were each different. I then asked some new questions: 'What percentage of the potential capacity of this leyline is actually running in it?' and 'How long has it been in place and running here?'

By using these questions repeatedly, a riveting series of answers emerged. Although some of these lines had been around for many thousands of years without changing their energy, the dowsing indicated that others of the energies present were brand new. Every energy numbered between one and seven had been in place since pre-history. Every line of a higher number was new and had only appeared in recent months or weeks. I re-measured specific lines from week to week. It became clear that every leyline had recently started to increase in energy and this process was continuing!

I continued with the dowsing to get specific answers about the new energies and asked, 'What energy was running in this line before the new energy?' and consistently got answers between one and seven. I also asked, 'If all the twelve cosmic building blocks are in place, will the thirteenth arrive?' and got a very clear 'Yes' from the crystal swinging over the chart, in reply.

These investigations and revelations took me up to about May of 1995. It was clear that the energies of the planet were all changing after many centuries of being fixed. There had, apparently for aeons of time, been seven, (or more accurately, six plus one) very weak energies, and now these were being replaced by thirteen, which had only just appeared, and were rapidly getting stronger. What was going on?

After much further research, I found systems of twelve-plus-one in many places across the planet – they exist in our mythologies, religions, senses, crystals, history, and many other places. Christ and the apostles were a good example, so were King Arthur and the Knights. The same archetypes appear amongst the Greek Gods, and again amongst the Roman deities, and are repeated in the mythologies of the Norse countries, the Vedic traditions of India – in fact everywhere I looked.

I then read a book which informed me that the chakra system, the energy system in the human body which conventionally has seven major centres in the body, was slowly being changed out for a system of thirteen, or more specifically, twelve plus one. So, did these tie up with the information I had compiled on the energy changes in the leylines? More dowsing on this line of enquiry revealed that indeed, they did!

What was becoming clear was that, at the energy level, we, individually, are each a direct reflection of the planet on which we live. It appeared that the energy system in the human body was also changing, in line with the energy changes in the planet.

The next significant development in this exploration occurred when a clairvoyant friend of mine, Dicky, called to tell me about a phenomenon called Herculobus. He had been given information that some kind of cosmic body, which appeared to be rather unstable, was travelling rapidly towards Earth. Since it appeared to be bigger than our planet, his mind, not unnaturally, turned to thoughts of the Apocalypse! I asked him a number of questions, and he went away to try and find answers. What Dicky came back with was that this body appeared to be changing at random from solid one moment, to an energy-only body the next; hence the instability!

At the same time I had been discussing the subject with a group on the Internet, an excellent source of data. Information poured in! In the middle of these exchanges, my friend Judy Crookes sent me an e-mail, asking if I knew anything about what she called 'Wormwood Consciousness'. I brought together all the e-mails and my insights, added it to the various bits of channelling, and then attempted to write down the totality of what was contained in all this information.

Here is my reply, which, by a process of synthesis, seemed to draw the whole thing together, so although it repeats some of what has been stated in the two previous chapters, I think it is valuable to re-state the whole. This, then, is what was circulated amongst our Internet group…

Dear Judy,

You ask about 'Wormwood Consciousness'. In order to come up with answers I have done a long dowsing sequence, and tied in (and checked) some of the things I already know, so as to complete an overall picture. I am somewhat stunned by what has emerged, am still integrating it, but here it is anyway!

I hope this story resonates for you!

Wormwood is part of a phenomenon I have been endeavouring to understand for some months. It is an aspect of something known as Herculobus, which is 'almost a planet', and consists ONLY of the higher dimensional levels (4th dimension and up) usually associated with a planet, for very good, historical reasons, which I will explain below.

It is all about the energetic effects of the fall of Atlantis. By the time that Atlantis developed on Earth, the planet was fully expressed in all its dimensions – in energy terms, it was much more than the mere three-dimensional planet we know. The spin of the planet enabled it to draw massive amounts of energy from higher dimensions (a process called transdimensioning), and feed it to the planet and its population by a highly activated Earth energy grid. Both the planet and its population were at significantly higher frequency than we are today.

After aeons of successfully working with the grid and the higher energies, the Atlanteans and their rivals, diverted and misused the grid energies. The human love of making war reared its very ugly head!

By using crystal technology, including vast energy storage devices and intensifiers, devastating weapons of war were developed that had all the power of atomic warfare and then some. Today's major deserts are largely a result of the damage caused by the use of these weapons. The Atlanteans fought and destroyed Lemuria, and also fought with the Vedic empire (in what is now the Indian sub-continent), and others.

The higher dimensions, and the energies that flowed from them, were controlled by various levels of the spiritual/angelic hierarchies. The earth energy grid was their gift, for the support of the human experiment. The abuse of the energies on Earth caused great concern. It became clear that the Earth itself was in grave danger of being destroyed, and the hierarchies therefore decided that their gift must be withdrawn: this meant that the higher dimensions of the planet had to be removed, since the potential destruction that was now looming would affect far more than just Earth, spreading as it would into the Cosmos at large.

It is probable that the destruction of Atlantis was a part of the plan to switch off the energies; in fact, in a channelling some time ago, we were told that Atlantis was BOTH the name of the civilisation, and the name of the Earth grid. The Atlanteans had full control of the global grid, and it gave them many powers (such as the ability of the priests and scientists to project to any point on the Earth, via the grid).

After Atlantis had largely been destroyed, a small group of the highly spiritual Atlantean priesthood, who had never supported the warring factions of their nation, were sent by the hierarchies to travel the Earth, and use their spiritual powers to switch off each vortex. These vortices were powerful and could be clearly seen, like tongues of fire in a furnace, multi-coloured and forming an upward facing 'cup' shape. The Atlanteans charged with the task of de-commissioning, had to walk right into the centre to close the vortex down.

After the vortices were de-commissioned, the higher frequencies of the planet, held together by the planetary grid, were detached completely from the planet. A second 'near planet', consisting of only the higher dimensions of the Earth was created as a separate entity, and went off into space, in its own orbit.

The Earth together with humanity, lost its higher energy support, and both slipped down the energy frequencies, steadily losing contact with their higher selves, guides, the hierarchies, et al.

This process was what the Bible refers to as THE FALL and this was indeed the effect of the steady downward path through the energy frequencies, and a resulting detachment from all that is spiritual and godly, along the way.

The detached higher-dimensional planet is that entity known as Herculobus containing the energies collectively known as Wormwood. Every two thousand years it has come into conjunction with the physical Earth, but on each occasion, humanity has not been ready to receive this gift of high energetic support. On the last occasion when Herculobus was in physical conjunction with this planet, Christ came to Earth, to seed new energies which would eventually enable humanity to go back up through the energy spectrum. This process is what is known as the ASCENSION. It is approaching us right now, and the planet, and we (at the energetic level) have been affected by it for some years, as things have started to change.

The Earth energy grid has, over the last year, increased its energy flow by almost 100 times, as it starts to resonate with the approaching Herculobus. According *to my measurement of the leylines, together with some recent channelling, these leylines are now almost at their 3-dimensional capacity, and will flip into higher dimensionality shortly. According to my dowsing today, Wormwood will be in full conjunction with the physical planet within about two weeks from now. These phenomena are clearly one and the same thing! This major energetic event is now right on top of us, so expect some interesting phenomena!*

This new (or renewed) energy grid will cause some initial stress to the planet, as things adjust and come into harmony. We have been feeling this stress in recent weeks. However, once in place, it will become a protection for the planet, though the speed at which this happens will be determined by the rate at which humanity develops its consciousness. As this process develops, as much as two-thirds of the negative energies of the planet have already been lifted off, to be replaced by this new, higher-dimensional and fully integrated energy. The remaining one-third will be removed after the grid has locked on to the planet for good.

So, Wormwood consciousness, is that consciousness which is created when humanity moves back up the frequencies; the consciousness of Ascension, moving us to multi-dimensionality (which we have to learn to manage if we are to expand into living with it). The arrival of these higher energies, which were always our (much delayed) birthright, gives us the potential to fully express the human blueprint for the first time since Atlantis. That human blueprint has changed very substantially since those times. We have integrated much as the wheel of incarnation has taken us on our downward journey. We are very different beings from the Atlanteans, and the human blueprint now has great reserves of wisdom and power.

Wormwood, according to the dowsing, is also the base for many etheric entities that used to be a normal part of human life. Many of our guides, or higher aspects of ourselves, use this as their base in some way. So, this is also a great re-union!

If this information is correct (and I have little reason to doubt it), both the energetic structures, and the opportunity for mass Ascension, will be fully in place within a few days. Hopefully, we are now ready for Wormwood to lock on to the planet, restoring its higher dimensionality permanently. This will be the start of a new process, with the potential to take us to a new range of possibilities, as we move to higher frequencies.

There has been a purpose to all of this, which has firstly been the development of the human blueprint, through a long process of tempering, to take human potential to a higher level. The other humanoid races have all, largely expressed their potential, and in terms of both spirituality, and technology, stand well ahead of us at the moment. We, however, have free will, new (still mostly latent) faculties, and the integrated effects of much human experience as a result of (in many cases) thousands of lives on Earth.

We shall, over time, develop to occupy the physical galaxy, and use our expanded powers to lift many other humanoid races above aeons of warring and territorial dispute (mirroring life on Earth for thousands of generations). Our potential, and that of the faculties and energies that we will begin to develop, will lead us through a huge metamorphosis. The 'end game', as it were, is no less than the redemption (or spiritualisation) of the physical universe! Enjoy the ride!

How long it will take humanity to grasp this one?

Best wishes,

Peter

So, it seemed that this Herculobus was the energy body that had been detached from the planet at the fall of Atlantis. It was the true energy grid – what had been left on planet Earth was just a magnetic shadow of the real energies. There was still a grid here, but energised to only a tiny fraction of what the full grid was intended to be. And the Herculobus body held the higher dimensions of the planet, which most other planets have, and which clearly add a great deal to the experience of the inhabitants, compared with a planet that is simply three-dimensional.

As Herculobus approached the planet, the 'resident' leyline grid began to resonate with the approaching 'real' grid. My increasing awareness of this led to the uncovering of a far more significant body of information, which showed much about the journey of humanity over some thirty thousand years since the highest days of long-lost Atlantis. All of this, which I had found to be intensely interesting, seemed to affirm that I might just have some skills as a geomancer, and thus perhaps, confirm the Hermes connection. It has been a huge adventure!

TRANSITION

Now
The past
Takes leave at last
To journey back,
        home
To the land
Of Everything-Before-It-Comes-To-Be.

        Now
We are crossing over
Into a quite new day
Which does not owe a thing
To what has been so far:

        For
Leaving countless woebound histories behind,
The time has come
For all the glories
                that could ever be
To find their way
                and make the break
        into concrete
Reality!

Chapter Ten

Miracles Of Healing – The Philip Story

An Angelic Prediction

In September of 1995, our friend Neris channelled some information directed towards Oonagh and myself. It told us that 'soon, you will be asked to do something of significance'. As always, we failed to spot that this was the start of another spiritual adventure, and a learning experience for many, many people.

The message was from Asphondel, an angelic being who I had experienced several times over the previous two years. When I first visited Neris, I was surprised when I recognised the Asphondel energy in one of her children. Asphondel was known to me as a very fine being (see Chapter 13), an Angel of the Dark, charged with the responsibility of bringing the light and dark together in the coming time of integration! Neris said later of Asphondel "He has absolutely no bedside manner" but is a being of great integrity, focus and purpose. The only other person of my acquaintance who carries this Asphondel energy I knew to be a wise and spiritually expanded man, who had been shocked when he learned of his energetic credentials.

The idea of who Asphondel is might frighten many, but our experience with him has been entirely positive. It gave yet another clue that the human concept of 'good and evil' is just that; a human concept. We had by this time formed the view that Light and Dark are a natural and necessary part of the physical plane of existence. We humans have raised the game, invented (and practised) a polarised Good and Evil, and in many respects, manifested exactly that phenomenon. Meanwhile, the angels from either hierarchy were simply following the wish of All-That-Is. Asphondel was to feature strongly in the coming adventure.

Soon after her introduction to Åsphondel, through my recognition of that energy being present in her son, Neris started to be visited by him, and experienced a number of direct conversations and strongly informing dreams. Now, in one of these, he sent information directly for us, and went far further than the initial prediction. This is what Neris recorded at the time, 22nd September 1995:

"Tell Peter and his partner that very soon they will be asked to work together in something that will be of great significance to this process you have all been engaged in...It will draw on their energies to the utmost but they must give and give selflessly and much will be given them. They will unite a network behind them...they may if they wish use the one who is the Holy Spirit in their work, or they may work between themselves and act as the lens through which the energies of so many people will be focused."

The Accident

We had no idea what this meant at the time, but in fact the "something" we would be asked to do started about two months later, on a Monday morning in November 1995. I had been working for an hour or so, when the phone rang. It was my friend Nick. "Hi, Nick," I said, full of Monday morning enthusiasm, "How are you?"

"I feel dreadful..." and then came the devastating follow-on, "...Philip's been in a car accident, and he's in intensive care."

Philip is Nick's son. A thirty-year old, 'go-getting' sort of man, who had a very successful career as an area manager in the courier business. Philip was 'driven' in all aspects of his life. However well he did, he always wanted to do better. Married for six years, full of life, forever pressing on, and driven by an inner turmoil that always seemed to show. Although I did not know him well, I could not imagine Philip in the deep coma that Nick described.

Philip was known as a careful driver, very 'laid back' and never driving in a reckless way. He had been going out to dinner the previous Saturday night, driving in the outer lane of a three-lane road, when his four-track vehicle suddenly swerved across two lanes, touched another vehicle, and they both went off the road. It appeared, after the event, that a third vehicle was probably involved, and may have struck Philip's car from behind first, but the real cause of the accident was never clearly established. The other car rolled over into the ditch, the occupants distinctly undignified as they hung upside-down in their seat belts, shaken but unhurt. Philip's car however, was a different matter...

The car rolled over at high speed, eight or nine times, and was completely annihilated in the process. Later, the police were to say that the only part of the vehicle they could identify was the petrol tank. Given the total destruction involved, nobody could have survived such an accident; but they did. Annie, Philip's wife, miraculously held in place by her seat belt, had a torn left ear which a few stitches would soon deal with, and general bumps and bruises. Even though he was still alive, Philip had not fared nearly so well. He had been thrown through the closed sunroof of the vehicle, and landed some fifteen feet in front of the now stationary remains of his 'wheels', apparently landing on the back of his head, in the road.

The prognosis was severe brain damage, as well as more than one broken vertebrae at the base of his spine, and such severe bruising to his rib cage, with attendant broken ribs, that later the effects of shock would cause his heart to stop.

Moments after the accident, the miracle began (there is no other word to describe the ensuing sequence of events). In the traffic close behind Philip, there were – in three cars, and quite unrelated to each other – the main components of a complete rescue team, who, by chance or design were there at the moment they were needed. Two American doctors on vacation were in one car. Another held a senior surgeon, on his way to go on duty at the local hospital. Finally, the local head of traffic police, now off-duty, drew up within moments, carrying a complete set of communications equipment on board his vehicle.

Things moved very quickly, and within an hour, Philip was in the intensive care unit of the local general hospital. He was assessed, stabilised, and placed on a life support system. However, this hospital accident unit could not cope with the needs of a severely brain-damaged patient, so soon after the initial assessment, he was transferred to the Atkinson Morley hospital, some twenty miles away, which has a trauma unit specialising in brain damaged patients.

At the Atkinson Morley, 8 am on Sunday morning, Philip underwent his first operation to remove a blood clot at the base of his brain, in order to relieve the pressure on it. If this had not been done, he was given a mere two hours to live! Even so, the prognosis as to his recovery was 'very slim'. His vital signs were all critical – for days the pressure in his brain remained well above the level that normally causes a complete failure, and subsequently, death. He was injected with a wide variety of drugs to stabilise him and had many monitors and breathing devices attached to his body.

By the time I received the call from Nick, the prognosis was very poor. Although the specialists at the hospital were very gentle in their handling of the situation, it was clear that they expected Philip to survive for no more than a couple of days.

The 40-day Note

Over the years, Nick and his wife Paula heard about some of the 'strange' (to them) spiritual things Oonagh and I were doing, and the many understandings that we came to as a result. Nick regarded us as generally crazy, but believed we were sincere in what we did, while Paula was rather more open to such possibilities. Now, Nick said to me, "I don't care if it is crazy. If there is anything you can do, please do it." In his extreme anxiety, he was willing to try anything.

I took Nick at his word, and began with some crystal dowsing, my method of asking questions about a situation to assess what is going on, and what options were available. I asked many questions about Philip. A startling picture emerged: the essence of the dowsing said that in 40 days, Philip would be substantially recovered! The net effect of my many questions was very clear about this. But what did it mean in the context of his current, seemingly hopeless position, and what needed to be done? On Tuesday 31st October I wrote a note to Nick, Paula and Annie, which said:

Our information is that Philip has a high chance of a full recovery: however, it may take up to 40 days before he regains full consciousness. If this occurs then the long delay is beneficial since major healing will be proceeding, uninterrupted. There are several indications that there needs to be a dialogue, which I need to discuss with you.

The situation remains very delicate and dangerous, so this cannot be simply taken for granted. The positive support of you, his family, is of great importance.

You need to be aware that he will almost certainly be able to hear what you say, probably see you and even experience your feelings when you are with him, and possibly even when you are away from him. It is important to talk to him in positive terms, to help his will to come back into consciousness when the time is right. It is very important to keep any individual fears, weeping, inter-personal stress or histrionics away from him because it may have a negative effect on his returning.

Just how do you deliver a message like that to parents and friends who are expecting someone to die imminently? The answer, as Nick was to say very much later, was 'like walking on glass'. The cruellest thing I could do was to give false hope. At the same time, I knew that if the message remained undelivered, then its effect would be negated. Feeling both nervous and foolish, I delivered my note with great care.

All that week, Philip lay completely inert. Not the faintest twitch, and all the time covered with tubes wired up to a battery of monitors, and with a ventilator breathing for him. Superficially, he looked fit and healthy, as if he were malingering. Only when you saw the massive surgical scar, and the enormous swelling and bruising down the back of his head, (the scar looking like some huge zip), did it really bring home to you just how serious his condition was. And it was clear that his soul, the real Philip, was simply not there.

Not really knowing where to go from here, and having no previous experience of such a situation, we decided to have a channelling session in search for more guidance, and to consult with the Quazar Council over the situation with Philip. We organised some quiet time, and got to work. This is the transcript of the conversation:

Peter: Quazar, you know we have been attending the place where the human being known as Philip Aston is, and that he has been involved in a serious accident. Is it possible for you to connect us to him, or relay him to us in some way?

Quazar: We can speak with him for you, and he can speak to you through us. We can also communicate with his angelic self. He is a being of enormous light and stature; such a beautiful, beautiful being, one who it is an honour for us all to serve.

Peter: Quazar, why is it that he has been in such turmoil during his life here on Earth so far?

Quazar: He has not yet come to terms with his purpose and role on this Earth at this time. He has been struggling to embrace the enormous love that he has all around him, and to allow it to flow through him. He cannot believe his luck in being so blessed, family-wise.

Peter: Has he been incarnated as a human being frequently?

Quazar: Indeed, and his last lives have been so traumatic that his soul does not know how to handle such a blissful existence.

Peter: Is this accident, then, purposeful in some way?

Quazar: Indeed, it was time for him to be called to order, to be reminded of his true reason for being here, of the agreements he has made, and what he is now to accomplish.

Peter: Quazar, would you please tell us about those agreements?

Quazar: *He is here to be a clarion call for the next move of energy-form into this planet. He is a bringer of the dawn, a leader of the light, a master of ascension.*

Peter: *Can you say more about this please?*

Quazar: *His role is to be like that divine image of the mandala of the lotus petal, which is informing all those that meditate and communicate with the divine through the Buddhist way. He is here to be like that lotus flower for the West, a mandala for the West to look at, and to see, and to understand all that is.*

Peter: *What is the energy that comprises his soul?*

Quazar: *He is one of those beings that is a total integration of all thirteen archetypal energies, as you understand them in your system.*

Peter: *It appears from our information that he does wish to stay on the planet at this time. Is that correct?*

Quazar: *Indeed. This is your great challenge. This challenge for you, and for Oonagh, is beyond any that you have experienced before. You are faced with people you love very deeply, who are not of your life, of your karma, of your previous lives. They are new souls in your experiential existence in this world. However, they are people you have formed a deep and truly meaningful relationship with, as you say in your jargon.*

Now, they are suffering in ways that you can feel enormous empathy for. Now, all that you have learned and all that you have known for some time is being put to the test. You have the opportunity to demonstrate your power, Peter and Oonagh, and you may either do this, or not according to your wishes.

Peter: It is clear from our dowsing that Philip wishes
to remain here, but at the moment he is so
detached from his body that he cannot find his
way back. Is it proper for us to seek ways to assist
him, since it is his wish to come back?

Quazar: Yes, and at all times remember it is not quite
what it seems. He is floating, as you might say,
away from his body, elsewhere in the Universe,
performing the functions and tasks, and gaining
the teaching he most needs to be the superior
light being for this planet. And this learning
period is most important for him. It would be
wrong to always, in this period, be calling him
back, through memorial services, or memorial
lighting of lamps.

Peter: Quazar, who is the highest being that we can
call upon, that will hold the light, and the energy
for Philip during this period while he is away
from his physical body?

Quazar: You and Oonagh would be best. You can do
this, and hold the merkabah present at all times.
It does not require enormous amount of energy,
you just need to check the structure at frequent
intervals to make sure that it is still intact.

Peter: Now, we need to find some way to demonstrate
to the medical staff, that there is life, more than
just his inert state, so that they will keep him on
life support, and his physical body protected.
How can we go about that?

Quazar: You will have to draw near to him, and breathe
life into him, as he breathes life into his own
body. In and out, breathing, feeling. Him feeling,
you breathing, you breathing, him feeling.
Slowly, within weeks of your time, you will see
some marked improvement.

Peter: How long, in our time scale, might we expect him to be unconscious?

Quazar: That is really a 'how long is a piece of string' question! It all depends how quickly he makes up his mind.

Peter: Would you then ask Philip what support he would like specifically, from us, and from the network who are with us?

Quazar: Of course. And we have already done this elsewhere. There is no difference here from what you have been doing elsewhere.

At this point we lost connection with Quazar, but it left us with much to think about. Here was the challenge, the 'something' we would be asked to do that had been foretold two months earlier.

The next morning, I called John Frank, who is a clairaudient friend of ours. We have worked with him over many years, and he has the most extraordinary ability. Normally, we just give someone's name, ask him for a sort of status report and then ask questions. I called John to ask for further input on Philip. John works with a committee of five discarnate beings. His speciality is giving profiles on people, simply having been given their name and no other information. On this basis (and bearing in mind that both Philip, and his condition, were completely unknown to John) this is what he gave me:

Date: 30th October 1995

Q. John, please give me a profile of Philip Aston.
A. He is basically very sound, but has been in one hell of a mix.
Q. Please explain?

A. He has had a very turbulent inner life. He never knows quite which face he is going to present to the world. He is only vaguely aware that he presents many different faces.

Q. Please tell me about his status right now?

A. He feels quite calm. He thinks he has lucidity of judgement and feels conversant with all the facts of the situation. This is not totally the case, because he is viewing the facts from a place that causes him a variable distortion.

Q. From where is he viewing the situation?

A. In general his perception is like having letters printed in red and black, and then viewing them through a red screen; the reds disappear, leaving only the black. In the same way there are some facts which he literally does not see.

B. Is he viewing from in his body or out of his body?

A. He is mostly in his body, but he flips between the two. I need to say that they (this refers to John's committee) like him enormously, he is thoroughly sound and his integrity is absolute: an all round good egg.

Q. Can we go back to his current status? How he is right at this moment?

A. He is in a very clear and lucid space at this moment — no longer fooling himself now, he has a good grasp of the facts of his situation, and of the connectivity of the facts.

Q. What is his degree of commitment to staying on the planet?

A. He is wavering.

Q. Why?

A. He feels called elsewhere. There is a conflict of loyalties between sticking around or moving on. He has had representations about his future role, some form of communications in another plane. (Note: only at this point did we tell John who Philip is, and describe the situation following his car accident).

Q. Does Philip have a choice about staying here or leaving?

A. Yes, he does.

Q. Will absent healing assist him?

A. Yes. His soul needs to engage in a dialogue about staying. His higher self can heal him if it and he choose that he stays.

Next, we proceeded to dowse with a crystal to provide responses to questions, to determine the potential effectiveness of several healers known to us, to see who might help. We tried a total of 16 people, asking who would be of most benefit to Philip in terms of their healing power and ability to assist him to return to a fully healthy and active life on Earth. Expressed as a percentage of 100, several scored between 75% and 90%, the latter being Oonagh and I working together. Our elderly friend, healer and prolific poet David Hadda scored 100%.

We phoned David, and he did some absent healing work in conjunction with some of his healing network. This is equivalent to a powerful 'laying on' of hands but done by the group from wherever they happen to be at the time, which can have a powerfully beneficial effect. David also agreed to come to the Hospital and work on healing support for Philip, if this was acceptable to the family. We knew that for the healer, being present is almost always more effective than absent healing. In effect, David, as the healer present with Philip would focus all the energies of those others actively giving healing support from remote locations.

Next we called upon our small, but powerful global network of highly spiritual people, and asked them to do absent healing, prayer, or whatever they could to assist. Because of who they are, they will all have done this immediately on request, and without necessarily replying, but we also had a few replies which gave us further information about the situation. In our experience, once a group like this has been connected energetically, the form of energy support it provides is actually continuous, flowing over perhaps months, until it is no longer needed.

In hospital, Philip had crowds of visitors. He was well liked, and so are his parents, but the degree of interest and the number of people who were expressing a concern for him was phenomenal. For the weeks that he was there, there were always people in attendance. In the first few days, the waiting room was full to overflowing. Even though Philip's situation was so serious, it was like a party, with all these people here to support him, caring, and in many cases, praying for him. We decided to enrol the energetic help of all these people. We knew that if co-ordinated, the effect of their energy would be massive. Lisa, a relative of Philip's mother Paula, who is also a spiritualist) activated her own network, so that perhaps 150 people became involved in providing energy support to Philip. Hardly anyone, spiritual or not, objected. We sent the following note to a large number of visitors; colleagues, tradesmen, fellow staff, school friends as well as friends of Philip's parents, relatives etc:

2nd November 1995

Energy Support for Philip

As a result of his car crash, and the trauma that came with it, Philip's soul – the real person – is disconnected from his physical body. The soul is indestructible, unlike the physical body, and it is widely believed that human souls pass through many lives on Earth, in a journey of learning and experience.

So, at the moment, the real Philip is in the form of pure energy. He will have little, if any, sense of time or place, and may well be very disorientated.

Through a technique called 'dowsing', we believe that:
* it is Philip's wish to return to his body;
* that, although this is not supported by any logic based on his physical situation, there is a very high chance of his fully regaining consciousness;
* that it may take up to 40 days for him to do this and
* that for the moment he cannot find his way back into his body; and if he could he may not yet be ready to return.

Since he is currently in energy form, the only real support we can give him is energetic. Every human being is a powerful energy source, but in our materialistic world we have mostly forgotten these powers (which are actually more important and enduring than our physical bodies). Together, then, we can harness these energies and set out to create an energy miracle. The request is that every person who is willing to support Philip at this time, should assist with three energy processes, which are described fully in the rest of this note, and are:

1) To provide him at his soul level with a continuing supply of energy to sustain and energise him in his current disconnected state.

2) To provide a beacon, so that he can literally find his physical body when he chooses to and the time is right; and to protect him in the interim.

3) To provide clear and positive thoughts to assist whatever process or journey he is presently going through.

Here is what you can do, to help create an energy miracle:

The following is an invocation (simply a prayer without any religious overtones). It is suggested that you find a quiet place to say this without interruption, while focusing on Philip – if you can do it by his bedside, so much the better, but it is not vital to be there. Please note that the effect of more people doing these processes is exponentially cumulative (i.e., the more people the better!).

The Invocation: (Note: at the * you may add the names of any religious or cosmic beings you pray to, or feel connected with, as feels right to you).

"I call upon my higher selves, my guides and guardians (*) and all those beings in the Universe who are of positive and integrated energy, to be here and support me in consciousness, so that through me divine energy now flows to support Philip at this time of choice and healing.

I offer myself as a willing channel for healing and supporting energies, and I ask to receive 110 percent of the energy transmitted to Philip, so that I shall be invigorated by the process, and not drained by it.

Philip, I open my heart to you, and I send you this gift of supporting and healing energy, as a continuing flow for as long as you may require it, and for your highest use. I know and accept that the choice and the decision to return to your body is yours. I unconditionally love and support you, in all your power and radiant magnificence, and regardless of what choices you now make. SO BE IT!"

It does not matter if you mix up the words. But please send loving, positive energy unconditionally, with no heavy pleas or angles!

It is vital that, as a communication, it comes from your heart. If it is just 'ritualised' it will not really be effective. The last sentence is the most important, and can be repeated whenever you find yourself thinking of Philip.

The Beacon

The purpose of this is to protect Philip's physical body, and give him his bearing when and if he chooses to return to it.

Imagine an energy construction, in the form of two triangular-based pyramids, completely surrounding Philip's body. The first pyramid is upright, the base under his bed, with one side along the back wall, and the point out towards the nurses desk. The second is inverted, with the 'base' above the bed, and one side parallel with the foot of the bed, on the same vertical axis as the first. Both pyramids enclose Philip completely.

With your eyes closed, imagine this structure into being. It is created of integrated, positive energy, impenetrable to any unwanted entities, and filled with golden-white light. This energy body acts as a reservoir for the energies you are sending through the invocation. Imagine both pyramids spinning, faster and faster, in all directions, becoming a sphere made of two blurred, spinning pyramids. As you do this, the energy body is energised, and becomes multi-dimensional so that it will reach out to whatever dimension and place Philip is currently in. After a little time imagining this construct, say the following:

"I dedicate this energy body as a protection for Philip's physical self, as a reservoir of supporting and healing energy for Philip to use as he wishes, and as a beacon so that he may find his way back to the physical plane. I call upon you, Philip, to connect with it and draw from it. SO BE IT!"

204

You might like to refresh this image whenever you have a moment.

Finally, provide positive thoughts. You are each in communication with Philip, at some level. Now, more than at any other time, he can hear your thoughts and experience your feelings. Try not to focus on thoughts and feelings which may not be assisting Philip at this time and may even have a negative effect.

Your emotions (e-motion, or energy-in-motion) are really important, and should not be suppressed. This exercise is simply to give you something positive and helpful to focus on, which will assist both you and Philip.

So, please try not to make any specific requests or demands on Philip, or direct strong emotions toward him, or go through remorse/anguish/blame or whatever other strong feelings you may have, but just concentrate specifically on the invocation and beacon above, and in general on loving, positive support.

The combined effect of the invocation, the beacon, and positive loving support is that everyone is doing the same positive thing in energy terms. This is vitally important, since it represents the only level of consciousness by which Philip can connect with us all at the moment. In the Bible, Jesus says he will be present 'when two or more are gathered together in my name' – this is, in effect, what we are doing, invoking divine energy. By understanding the situation in energy terms, we can unite to send out a clear, positive and robust energy message, which will give Philip vital support that he can make great use of. The positive energies of our Universe will join in!

We all have the power of healing, together!

Please copy this note, pass it on and ask anyone who is willing to join in this energetic action to support Philip.

To Pull the Plug?

At the end of the first week, with no noticeable progress, Philip was still on full life support. Friday, two weeks after the accident, the consultant doctor was to review whether there was any progress, on which evaluation would ultimately rest the decision as to whether to discontinue life support, and simply let Philip die naturally. Nothing that represented progress on Philip's part had happened, and we were all praying for just some small sign of movement; something that would encourage the consultant to stay his hand, and give more time for the work we, and many others, were doing to take effect. The consultant inspected Philip with care, after which he said, "Well, Philip is a very fit young man, and miracles DO happen" and with that, postponed his decision until the following Monday. In the event, he was called away on the Monday, so the decision was delayed again, to Tuesday. By then, Philip had started to stir; some part of his soul had, indeed, come back into his body.

Since the messages from the Angel Asphondel, I had offered to be a conduit for all the energy pouring in from the CompuServe group, and all the others that were offering their energetic support. The effect of this on me was very marked: when Philip had a crisis, I was energetically wiped out, and had to retire to bed for several hours, sleeping heavily when I did so. This happened several times during the whole episode. As his brain started the healing process, I had this constant crawling feeling in my brain. And when he started to move, I also felt it. One day in the second week, I was sure he was trying to move his eyelids and wanted to know if this was indeed the case. Excited, I rang Nick at the hospital in order to check, only to be told "You'll never guess what: his eyelids are moving!" before I could get my request in!

Now, Philip was moving a lot, wriggling in the bed, and, dangerously, pulling various cables and tubes off himself, but he was still unconscious. Talking to Nick, who was spending hours by Philip's bedside (as were all his closest friends and relatives, in relays), I suggested that he stop conversing, and start putting out a simple question, "Can you hear me, Philip? If you can, please give me a signal." I cannot imagine how many times Nick must have asked, but when I visited the following day, he told me "I'm sure he is trying to move his eyebrows in response to me." The following day I was told, "His response is getting stronger, and now one of the nurses has seen it!"

The next morning, incontrovertible proof! On being asked the oft-repeated question, Philip gave a 'thumbs up' sign with his left hand. Having been asked to do the same with his other hand, the right thumb went up. Two things were absolutely clear: Philip was back in his body, and both sides of his brain were now working, to some extent. Over the next few days, there was rapid progress. More signalled communication. One eye was opening, and he signalled that he could see, if only vaguely. While I was there and watching on one never-to-be-forgotten day, Philip suddenly leaned up from his bed and hugged his mother, Paula. I was moved to tears as I watched from the far side of the ward unbeknown to Paula – the miracle we had asked for was working! Soon after, Philip started to communicate by mouthing words (there was no sound because of his tracheotomy), at first in a very unclear and hesitant way, and then with increasing coherence.

Shortly after the 'thumbs up' incident, it became clear to the doctors that Philip was suffering from hydrocephalus; water being generated around the damaged area of his brain, which had started to create great, and potentially dangerous, pressure. It was decided to operate, and insert a device called a 'Shunt'. This is a small tube which is inserted in the cranial cavity, and passes down through the body to some convenient overflow point; in this case, Philip's abdominal cavity. X-rays had shown that the left frontal lobe of Philip's brain was particularly damaged, so that this was where the upper end of the shunt was inserted. Medical opinion seemed to be that the damage here was too severe for the brain tissues to regenerate, so in effect, insertion of the shunt at this point could do no more damage.

At that time, Oonagh and I went to a supper with about 40 people from the 'Through Heart to Peace' women's group, who had been going in and out of Bosnia during the height of the fighting, giving support to people there in many ways. At supper, we sat with a therapist who specialised in remedial therapy for those who had suffered Philip's kind of accident. We told her about the case, and she gave us several useful pointers as to what might be expected. She said that the demand for intensive care beds meant that the major risk would come when Philip was moved. It would almost certainly be to another hospital, and it was essential that they could provide the relevant care. Since we knew all the options, we ran these by her, and at the mention of one particular hospital she exclaimed, quite vehemently, 'No way!' and went on to explain that the record of this hospital in her field was far from impressive. She gave us a few details. If she was accurate in what she was saying (and events were to prove her right), then she was correct to state that this hospital should be avoided for Philip's kind of needs.

We passed on the somewhat dire warning! The subject of moving hospitals came up within about ten days, and Nick rang to say that that Philip had been moved one Saturday night – to precisely the general hospital that we had been warned against! Philip was put in one of four intensive care beds at this hospital, but this hospital had no specific experience of his kind of injury, so that we were all somewhat wary of the situation. Worse still, the arrival of another accident victim within a few hours meant that the following day Philip was moved to an ordinary ward, under the care of a trainee nurse with many patients to attend to. Here, there was absolutely no understanding of the care necessary to support his condition, and in particular the action needed to keep the shunt from infection. Soon Philip – who still needed, but was not getting, constant attention – was in a dreadful condition; filthy dirty, with none of the intensive attention that his situation demanded.

Fortunately, Sonia, Philip's sister, is a trained nurse, as well as a strong-minded lady. She, and Philip's parents, made a great deal of fuss, and forced the registrar of the hospital to take an interest in this case, and improve things as best he could. The lack of experience on this ward was so apparent that Sonia ended up writing the care programme for her brother! Things improved and everyone made the best of a difficult situation.

By this time, Philip was awake most of the day, and talking more freely. There seemed little sign of the lower back damage which had originally been a major concern, and thought to be quite severe. One magical morning, he further surprised everyone by getting out of his bed, and, with a little assistance, walking the length of the small ward! Just to show it was not a fluke, he did it again the same afternoon. This demonstrated that his lower back was indeed healed.

However, this rapid progress was not maintained. Philip's shunt became infected. This was extremely serious, and he was rushed back to the Atkinson Morley hospital. The shunt was removed, and he was placed in isolation, as the infection was of the virulent MRSA virus, a form of infection which is a specific problem in hospitals at present, because this strain seems to have mutated so that it no longer responds well to drug treatment. A high proportion of the people who catch it simply don't survive.

For some days, Philip was once again in serious difficulty with a life-threatening infection, but after expert attention and recovery from the infection (very much against the odds) the enforced removal of the shunt was eventually to lead to yet another miracle. When the doctors were finally able to X-ray his head once again, there was no sign of the damage to Philip's right frontal lobe. Despite medical opinion to the contrary, the brain tissue had, indeed repaired itself. It was as if the infection had occurred so as to cause the shunt to be removed, and this removal had allowed the healing to take place!

From here, things steadily got better, and Philip progressed well. Nick and Paula went to see the senior consultant at the Atkinson Morley, and asked how Philip was doing, in view of the condition he had arrived in. The Senior consultant was quite clear in his reply, *"As far as I know, he is the sickest patient who has ever left here alive."*

New Healing Powers

After some weeks Philip moved to Kingston hospital

where he progressed rapidly, and was then discharged into a programme where he attended a remedial centre during the week, but went home at week-ends. But there was one more miracle yet to come, and it concerned not Philip, but his father, Nick...

In the days following the accident, Nick – who maintains that he is neither religious nor spiritual – had prayed intensely for his son's life, calling upon everyone in other realms that he thought might help. One of the beings he invoked was the soul of Ted Fricker, who had been a most accomplished, and celebrated healer. Fricker had been dead for several years, but had once cured Nick of a painful back condition, using healing energies, after conventional medicine had failed. Nick had been greatly impressed. Fricker then said to him, "If ever you need my healing ability in the future, just visualise my person and ask, and the healing energies will be available to you."

Ted Fricker had departed this earthly plane, but Nick did what he had suggested; he envisaged the healer, and called for his assistance. Perhaps Ted Fricker's great healing power joined with that of all the people sending energy to Philip, and played its part in the ensuing miracles...Many weeks later, Nick sheepishly confessed to me, "I have been hearing voices!". This came as a total shock to him! He described how he had run out into the street from his home, in an effort to get rid of this voice.

"Who do you think it might be?" I asked, and he replied, "This will sound really silly, at first I thought it must be God. Then I realised that it had an East End of London accent, and God would hardly call me 'my boy' in quite that way! I think what I am hearing is Ted Fricker." Amazing stuff! Even more so when we realised what Fricker had been saying to Nick.

Nick was told that the healing energy that Ted Fricker had been blessed with needed a new home now that Ted was gone; a human being who could learn to use this great gift, and carry on with the healing work, perhaps picking up where Fricker had left off. Nick had invoked Ted Fricker to help in healing Philip, and now the healing gift was being offered to him permanently, if he would accept, and use it in service to others! The voice, he was told, would be available to assist in diagnosing those illnesses that this healing energy was able to help.

And this is what has started to happen. Nick clearly has a new faculty of powerful healing capability, and is growing in confidence as he begins to get some real results, helping those with illnesses who come to him whenever he can.

It seems to me that every stage of this saga has been, in some way, quite miraculous. It has illustrated that human and divine intervention when they work together, can 'beat the odds' of what we can ordinarily do and know in the conventional technologies of our physical world!

Although Philip made a truly miraculous recovery in the physical sense, he still had to undergo a long rehabilitation and at times this prolonged process was very trying for his loving and patient family. He was a completely different person after the accident, and part of his memory and some of his automatic functions were either missing or suspect. There was much that he would have to re-learn, and it would be a long while before he was to be able to work again. Indeed, all the things you would expect after a major trauma. But the fact remains that, by all medical standards, he simply should never have survived at all!

HEALING

A healing
      must not stop the illness
      from revealing
The misuse
      of a part of life in us
We have been foolishly concealing.

All that we are
      and have on board
Is needed on our voyage,
      can only at our peril
Be ignored.

Chapter Eleven

The Power Of Manifestation

The power of Manifesting is another dramatic faculty we all possess, latently, but have mostly forgotten. To describe this power simply, manifestation is when you think sufficiently clearly and with intention about something, and then the particular thing in question *will start to happen.*

There are a range of techniques which can be used to assist in this practice, but the essence is very simple: you focus very clearly on what you wish to have come about, and ask the appropriate cosmic beings for their assistance.

A word of caution however! What you ask for using this technique appears to be far less likely to happen if it is self-serving, or if you keep changing your mind. Money, as a form of energy (in cosmic terms) appears not to be manifest-able directly. A group of people who are working on one common request is far more powerful than one individual, although it is surprising what one person can achieve! The most powerful requests are those that are framed in terms of 'I request this to come about in a way which will serve the highest good for the positive progress of humanity'. This seems to gain more attention at the cosmic level to which these requests are directed, and thus more energy is made available for their fulfilment.

The story that follows was when I realised that things were happening that I had thought about, and wished for, but had not yet acted on!

MANIFESTING AND AIRSHIPS

Right through the 1980s and early 90s in varying degrees of intensity, I have been involved in an amazing and on-going project, to develop large-scale Airships for volume production. This originally arose because I had been left a set of design calculations for such a craft, by the partner of a famous aeronautical designer, with the request (based on an interest I had

expressed some years earlier) that I should 'do something about it'! I brought together a small group who were interested in the project. We were subsequently able to show that the design I had been given was potentially a very inexpensive way to move goods – especially valuable in developing countries without an infrastructure of ports, rail or major airports. At the same time, the technologies being rapidly developed by the aerospace industries of the world meant that the airship-based system of transportation, for long a dream for many, might now become a practical and safe reality.

I therefore decided to keep the project moving slowly, and make what contacts I could with a view to progressing it. Over the years since this decision, the Airship project has involved so many inexplicable coincidences, and other extraordinary phenomena that it makes an interesting story and a natural for this collection! So here is what happened.

My involvement came about quite inadvertently in about 1984. I was invited to a house party thrown by friends who owned a large, rambling, Victorian farmhouse, hidden in a sleepy valley in Devonshire. I spent most of the weekend talking to an elderly gentleman, John Robinson, whose company I found highly congenial and whose conversation was absolutely fascinating.

In hindsight it was one of those meetings which were simply meant to be! John was the epitome of a typical 'mad professor', and even at his age (I believe he was in his early 80s) he had prodigious energy, talking at twice the speed, and with twice the knowledge of anyone else I know. He told me that in the late 1920s and early 1930s he had been an apprentice designer with two others, on the British airship R100. His colleagues were the celebrated novelist, Neville Shute, and the later-to-be-famous Barnes Wallis.

The R100 was eventually scrapped, after the disaster of the R101, which crashed on its maiden voyage, brought about by all sorts of political pressures which have been well-documented elsewhere.

In about 1980, Neville Shute, Barnes Wallis and John Robinson got together again for a long weekend reunion, during which they speculated about what might have happened to the Airship, if it had gone through all the stages of development associated with the Aircraft industry in the intervening fifty or so years. They then formulated a concept for a new genre of Airships, and they subsequently followed this up with quite a lot of work on the idea. I expressed great enthusiasm for the project as we talked; it seemed to me that the ideas they had developed were thoroughly viable, and exciting. John told me sadly that Barnes Wallis, the design genius behind the project, had subsequently died, so the momentum and indeed much of the 'heart' had gone out of the effort.

John Robinson and I had an in-depth discussion about all aspects of the project – the air was thick with talk of operational issues, propulsion, applications, materials, and handling considerations. Eventually, John broke off with a sigh, and said to me, "Look, I'm an old man now, and I doubt I will be able to do much more about it. If I were to send you the papers, would you promise to find a way to keep the idea alive?"

Without any hesitation as to what I might be taking on, I immediately agreed. Then, over the passing days, all memories of my commitment gradually faded. As it turned out, I was never to meet John Robinson again...

Months later, I was surprised to get a call right out of the blue from a woman, who turned out to be John's widow. In his will he had made the unusual request that she should ask me if I would still honour the commitment regarding the Airship project, and if I was of the same mind about this, she was to send me the entire body of his paperwork on the subject. There was no doubt whatsoever in my mind. I agreed instantly that I would do as he had originally asked.

A small mountain of paperwork arrived; mostly design and lift calculations, plus some descriptions of how the ship would function. This triggered my memory and brought to mind all that John had told me, including much technical detail, so I decided to use my PC and write up all that I knew, in order to have a base from which to start.

This I duly did, but at the time I had many other business pressures and commitments, and the papers and the report were soon consigned to the back of the filing cabinet. The report stayed there for about three years, but eventually I recommenced work on it with renewed enthusiasm. It was then that the many strange things associated with this project began to happen.

The first extraordinary incident took place when I went to a workshop organized by my clairvoyant friend, John Frank. He was doing some experimental work with a group of six people on advanced creativity, and the development of what John calls 'group brain'. This is a technique where everyone spends time focusing and meditating together, and achieving such a high degree of harmony that eventually, all those present start to share the same thoughts at the same time, with no external prompting. It's an amazing experience, although I found it a little frightening at first. Then, at one point during the day (and being highly sensitised because of the work we had been doing) I got the strong impression that there was an entity of some kind, an energetic presence in the room with us. This feeling grew in intensity, eventually building to a point where I felt compelled to mention it.

"Would you like me to find out who or what it is?" asked John who is always open-minded about such things. I asked him to proceed.

After a little time, he said "Well, this is very odd; this being says it was once the human called Barnes Wallis, and that he is here to support you in some project that involves you!"

John Frank had known a little bit about the project from past discussions, but nevertheless it was truly amazing that he had 'sensed' the presence of Barnes Wallis in the room. There was no question of my disbelief. Every instinct told me that John was on to something. This felt *right,* though entirely 'off the wall'! There was definitely a direction in all this...

As I proceeded with my work, I soon came to the conclusion that I was out of my depth. I realised that I needed help, since I had little in the way of technical skills, apart from my training in boat design, which helped considerably with some aspects of construction, and very basic aerodynamics. At about this time, I had begun to read about the technique of manifestation, which was basically supposed to work along the following lines: if you focused very clearly on something you wanted to bring about in every possible detail, and then asked the spiritual world to bring it to you, it *would* happen, usually very quickly. Having reached something of an impasse on the practical side of things I decided to try this technique in order to progress the Airship project. After all, what did I have to lose?

Looking at my priority of needs, I knew that I urgently required some information about Jet engines, and how they might be applied to this particular project. They had been envisaged by the Wallis team as an integral part of the overall design, and I needed to know rather more than my somewhat basic knowledge. Rather sheepishly, a bit self-consciously – and definitely with no one else present – I looked upward, and said something like, "Well guys, I understand you can help me if I ask clearly. Can you please find and bring to me a jet engine specialist, with knowledge which is relevant to the Airship project?" I well remember feeling rather foolish about doing this, but nevertheless went through with the process.

Three days later, a strange thing happened. A friend, Mick, who I had not spoken to for many months, rang me with a report about a mis-dialled phone call which, for some obscure reason, he thought might interest me. He had got a wrong number, and when the phone was answered, tried to apologise and ring off. "Who are you, anyway?" demanded a rather angry voice at the other end. Mick explained that his business was Insurance, and Project finance.

"Well," said the angry voice, now sounding just marginally less angry, "perhaps you can help finance the next stage of my latest project?"

They embarked on a lively discussion about what was needed. The upshot was that the project involved a technology design group of about twenty people, based in West London, using some very sophisticated Computer Aided Design systems to design...a large-scale and lightweight JET ENGINE, apparently perfect for the application I had in mind for the Airship!

Well, this was quite a turn-up for the books! Not only had the contact with this group been established BUT my friend Mick thought that I would be interested, on the flimsiest of evidence! I was quite surprised...what a coincidence, I thought, as I pondered after the event.

A few weeks later, a similar situation arose, but now I was in need of input on the subject of Aerodynamics, as my basic knowledge had long since been exhausted. Remembering the apparent success of the 'jet engine episode', and very much in the spirit of 'Oh well, why not...', I looked approximately heavenwards, and asked for expert help with Aerodynamics.

A bit later that week, I was asked to do some work for *The Hunger Project*, a strategic charity which I supported at the time. They were planning a major event in London, and asked me to make some liaison calls to assist with their plans. I worked through half a dozen calls, and found myself really enjoying dealing with a man called Geoffrey Pardoe. Our business completed, I asked, "By the way, Geoffrey, what exactly do you do for a living?"

"Oh," he said, "I'm the chairman of General Technology Systems."

"And what does the company do?" I asked.

"Well," said Geoffrey, "We are an international firm of Aerospace Consultants, operating in sixty countries."

"Great," I thought, "maybe I can make some progress on Airships!" and out loud I said, rather tentatively, "Geoffrey, do you think I might come and see you on an aerospace matter?"

An appointment was made, and I went along to the meeting, where I was shown into a spacious office, and met the very genial and helpful Dr Geoffrey Pardoe, for what turned out to be the first of many visits. But on this first occasion, somewhat nervously, I explained about the Airship project; where I had got to, and my current need for assistance with aerodynamics.

I finished my diatribe. There was a long silence, and a long, quizzical look from my new acquaintance. After what seemed an age, he said with some humour, "Well, you may be interested to know that my original discipline was aerodynamics. My personal passion is to be instrumental in bringing back large-scale Airships and GTS (his firm) has just completed a major study on the feasibility of this, for the UK Government."

Another 'hole in one'! I was beginning to be impressed by this manifestation technique!

However, there was to be a third in this series of out-of-the-ordinary occurrences, and this time, I was to be really quite shaken!

A few weeks further down the line with the project, a practical problem surfaced. One of the greatest problem areas in the practical management of Airships was the whole issue of ground handling. I needed someone with 'hands-on', if you'll pardon the pun, experience of a wide variety of such handling situations. Once again, I turned to the Cosmos – I was getting quite practiced at this – and duly asked.

Early the next week, I was to attend a board meeting of a company I had set up some years earlier. I arrived early, and found Tim, a good friend who represented one of the institutional investors on the board. We got chatting to kill time before the meeting.

"What are you doing now?" he asked. I muttered something about 'the usual crazy projects', to which he responded, "Well, we have half an hour before the meeting. Why don't you tell me about one of them?"

I filled him in briefly on the Airship project. At the end of my outline, he said, "I have a friend who is very keen on Airships. I'll put him in touch!"

I greeted the suggestion without excess enthusiasm, knowing that most enthusiasts and supporters of airships simply waste a lot of time looking back nostalgically to how things had been early in the century. This was emphatically not what the current project was about, so I did not really relish the call.

When it came, I was truly amazed. My caller and his brother ran an Airship Management company, operating up to nine airships commercially. They were the only people in the world currently doing this.

The Airship Project has continued to progress like that now for over ten years. Amazing things happen, apparently, on a wish. It's clear that someone 'up there' wants this project to happen. It continues to advance, so as the advertisers say, "Watch this space"!

So just how might we do this work? Here are some extracts from conversations with Quazar about the techniques required for manifesting:

Louise: Quazar, you said that requests are hollow if our thought patterns are not aligned with them at all times. Is this the secret of manifestation? I wonder why some things are so easy to manifest, and others so difficult. Could you comment on that please?

Quazar: Manifestation takes the requirement of the human form to focus energy in three ways. The first is intention. If it is not your 100% intention to manifest, really clearly that this is your full intention, you have no doubts about your desire to manifest this, and about your abilities, then you will manifest easily. The other aspects are with the intention, the will, and finally the love energy, the passion, the desire. All energies need to be harnessed in the human form in their manifestation...

And in another session, this came up:

Quazar: *What we are doing is creating, at the causal place, the image of what it is you wish to manifest. Then you can focus energy on that form and bring it into the three-dimensional planes, trusting that as you focus, you will attract all the pieces of the 'jigsaw' that are required to create and manifest this form.*

   We will assist you, because we need to assist with the creation of the image at energetic level. Then, when we have clear instructions from you to assist in the three-dimensional creation, we can hold the causal plane image too with you and remind you of it, and use it to plant in other people's minds as well, so that we all resonate with the energy of what you are manifesting.

Peter: *It seems to me that we are creating an energy that represents the outcome of the project; and that you being much closer to the energetic environment are able to hold that energy, grounded if you like in the causal plane, and then bring it into manifestation here.*

Quazar: *Well, once we have set up the energetic forms robustly, then we will learn what it is you need. Step by step, to create to flow into this energy form, and we will work with you then to do so.*

A while later, Oonagh and I had the opportunity to try out our manifesting techniques once again!

THE YELLOW CAR

It was spring 1994. Oonagh was well overdue to change her company car. She had wanted a convertible

four-seater for ages. I suggested several times that she looked at the Saab 900 model, but her only response was "I don't like Saabs," so we did not get very far! Then, on a trip to the west country, we drove past a Saab dealer, and there were two of the very model I had in mind sitting in the window. I drove straight in. As Oonagh saw the cars, she became enthusiastic. We took a test drive, and she was duly 'converted'!

We looked at the brochures. She decided on a top of the line model, a turbo in yellow, and said (somewhat to my disappointment) that she wanted an automatic. When we relayed her request to the garage, they said "Oh no, madam, this is the sports model. It is not made in an automatic model, although all the other models are," and tried to sell her something she did not want!

"That's OK," said Oonagh to me. "I'll manifest it!" This caused me a certain amount of rolling of the eyeballs. If this model wasn't made, surely no amount of manifesting would help. She talked to several dealers (unsuccessfully) and said "Just wait. We'll have it in a few days". "No chance," I muttered under my breath!

The other problem (also to be tackled in the manifestation) was that this model was about £6,000 over the company budget!

Then the impossible happened. One of the dealers rang to say that he had found the car! He had been to the UK office of Saab, and there was the very specification we wanted, sitting in the car park. A Saab director has ordered this car as a special, to evaluate its potential for the UK market. He had done only a few miles, and was ready to part with the vehicle when approached by the enterprising dealer! As a 'second-hand' vehicle, a significant discount was agreed, *and the car arrived at home just two weeks after Oonagh had done her manifestation work!*

In practice, we have had a number of examples of manifestation working for us, when we have applied ourselves to it. Indeed, we should really be convinced, and use it all the time. The practical difficulty is that it is so far removed from the normal human mind set of 'we must work at things, and struggle to organise people and resources to have things happen'! However, it seems to me that the rapidly changing energy environment around us – as discussed in earlier chapters – is bringing with it a changed environment where the power of the mind to create is greatly enhanced. I believe that we will soon start to find that a number of human faculties which have long been discussed and occasionally reported, will become far more commonplace. And many will find that, if they wish to develop such skills, it is open for them to do so. So, just maybe this magical stuff will soon be shown to have its practical applications, as well!

Don't send your prayers
Out into the blue
Merely on spec –
      in case there's something
Somewhere out in space to hear:
Without you sensing us,
We are ignored,
         passed by,
Till we ourselves
Can be no longer sure
That we are there – exist!

But anyhow:
Whether you're part of me
      or we of you
Or all of us
Components of a larger whole
We too – like you –
      must sometimes change our mind:
We can't stay blind
         to what
   till now
Was out of range for Man;
Just as for Spirit-kind.

So
Address your prayers
      without fail
More clearly,
      with a surer hand,
   or they might land up
Getting lost
In the celestial mail!

Chapter Twelve

Visitors From Other Dimensions

It has often been suggested to me that not all human beings we see around us is quite what they appear to be. This phenomenon can take several forms. There are those entities in some other realm who are relatively high beings (which usually refers to their level of responsibility, rather than some 'command' appointment), and have incarnated here for just a single visit. These people can be a little unworldly, as if they are not really used to being in a human body (which is, indeed, the case).

Then, there are those who are over-shadowed by a high energy being, so that the two join together to experience a single human journey. Christ was said to have been progressively overshadowed by ever higher beings, through his lifetime. Although these overshadowings are sometimes called 'walk-ins', they are mostly a human joining up with his or her higher self – that aspect which is cosmic in origins. Although it might seem a surprising thing to happen, there is a way in which this re-connection might be seen as quite natural…

And then, there are those who simply project themselves into our dimension from other realms. My first story under this heading just may have been one of those:

ANGEL VISITORS

In the early summer of 1991 we had two visitors. We didn't know them before they arrived, and though this sounds a bit vague, we were never *entirely* sure where they came from. They entered our lives, stayed with us for over three weeks, and disappeared as mysteriously as they had come. This is what happened...

An acquaintance who we had met for the first time at a gathering we attended the week before, rang us to say that two people, Victoria and Jersheirra, were arriving in London and would conduct a workshop on the subject of Ascension. This topic has been much discussed in the mid-nineties but at this time it was unknown and definitely not on anybody's agenda. What was being offered then was quite new and fresh. We were intrigued. Our contact also said these two needed somewhere to stay and he asked for our help in organising a second and if possible, subsequent workshops. So we volunteered...well, what else could we do, being such spiritually inquisitive people?!

I attended the first workshop, held in someone's attic in Clapham Common, which was beautifully converted into a large, well-lit, wooden-floored room with no furniture and a shrine at one end. We sat in an oval formation with Jersheirra and Victoria, and worked through the day at a high level of concentration. The material was certainly intense – they could have spent two or even three days delivering it – and we were introduced to many aspects of this new subject of Ascension. They explained that it was a process of metamorphosis that humanity was beginning to go through which was predicted in many ancient documents. They imparted a great deal of information that we had never heard before.

They were certainly extremely knowledgeable about their material. They explained the Cosmic hierarchy to us in great detail, informing us of how it worked, and they discussed the responsibilities of each level of this hierarchy. In particular, they talked about the responsibility for Earth and the human experiment as being the office of the Christ, and that the holder of that office for the last 2,000 years had been a being called Jesus Sonanda. He was, they said, in the process of handing over to the holder for the New Age, who is known to us as St. Germain. In addition, they described to us how Ascension would result in a rapid raising of our energy frequencies, and told us how diet, and internal bodily cleansing, would help us literally lighten our bodies, and raise our vibrations. There was much, much more along the same lines...

I came away excited, impressed, enlightened. I called a number of my more esoteric friends, enthusing about what I had heard, and put together a group for a second workshop a week later. At that time, my partner Oonagh had a house in Ealing which was large, airy and gracious. There was plenty of space there since Oonagh was by then spending most of her time with me on my houseboat on the river Thames, about five miles to the south. So Victoria and Jersheirra moved in there for the duration of their stay. And so the second workshop was held and was pronounced a great success.

Our boathouse by the river, a structure built in 1880, with stained glass windows and a carved wooden lining so that it resembles a small church, was now employed by Victoria and Jersheirra to give a number of one-on-one transformational sessions. These were quite extraordinary. Crystals were laid around the room (which had been cleared of its office equipment), sound equipment was installed and used to amazing effect. Victoria and Jersheirra worked with one person at a time for two hours in the most intense process. I can't recall all the details with much clarity but the energies flying around us were prodigious. I remember that there was a great deal of invocation and incantation, which quickly took me into a very altered state, more so than I had experienced at any previous time. I seemed to have many visions – in particular, I remember seeing a white Knight on a magnificent charger, standing quietly to my left as I lay on a blanket on the floor. I identified this being as some aspect of my father, who had died a year or so earlier.

Throughout the sessions, I was aware there was a tremendous amount of energetic activity going on in my physical self. Victoria and Jersheirra explained to us that a part of their process was to 're-encode the fire signs' in our bodies. This referred to elements of our physical and DNA make-up, which had been disabled aeons back in the development of humanity, and were now in the process of being reconnected.

They also explained to us that we would be subjected to a fair amount of physical side-effects from this work, over a number of future months. For instance, we might experience the onset of heavy cold or flu and yet never get past the initial stages; other symptoms might manifest as severe muscular stiffness and dizziness and weakness in the body, as well as a disabling tiredness which might cause us to sleep for several additional hours outside of our normal sleep schedule.

All of this sounds fairly alarming, and all of these things certainly happened. Several times I experienced being almost 'poleaxed' by tiredness. One moment I would be fully alert and functioning normally, the next totally unable to keep my eyes open, so that the only thing I could do was sleep; and this in the middle of the day! I found myself experiencing strange vibrations in my body, of a high frequency, and apparently moving from part to part, limb to limb, according to some schedule which I did not comprehend, but which I dimly knew was underway.

Another strange phenomenon I experienced was what I call 'physical dizziness'. If you can imagine the dizziness we sometimes get in our heads, but experienced only in the body, this will give you some idea of what was going on. As if this wasn't enough, in addition there were those times when I just seemed to disconnect from the planet and float off...!

Somewhat reassuringly, we were told by our two visitors that when these things started to happen, they were to be taken positively and regarded as signs of the physical body integrating higher energies that it was not used to. Later, when we compared notes with others, we became aware that the same things were starting to happen to many other people around us.

When we went through this transformational process it certainly seemed very positive, and any future side effects were seen as worthwhile. It was carrying us forward in some way, a potentially valuable part of our exploration. I remember, after the event, that I was joyously spaced for days...

In retrospect, I have to say that there was nothing particularly unusual about Victoria and Jersheirra. They were loving, gentle human beings, very positive in what they had to say; totally supportive, and extremely knowledgeable on the subject of Ascension, the coming change for the whole of humanity. They were a joy to be around! The one slightly unusual thing was that they always wore white, not flowing robes, but items like white T-shirts and white jeans perhaps. Since it was early summer this was only marginally unusual and they always looked spotlessly clean. They were a delight to have with us, and their energies always seemed to brighten up and enhance the environment we were in. Yet there was something about them...but I could never put my finger on just *what* it was...

Towards the end of their visit I settled down with them one evening at the house in Ealing when no one else was around, and asked quite directly, "Who are you – really...?" They looked at each other for a few moments...then looked at me...and looked back at each other.

There was quite definitely some sort of acknowledgement and exchange going on between them and after a fairly extended pause, Jersheirra turned to me and said, somewhat sheepishly, "Actually, we are rather minor angels. We have incarnated on this planet specifically to start the discussion amongst humanity about Ascension..." Victoria then added in a matter-of-fact tone, "We have served in many other places in the cosmos. On different planets, and on what you call UFOs – really, for us, this is just another assignment, although one that we are enjoying enormously! We have always wanted to be here..."

Well, despite the 'mind-boggling' aspects of their revelations, my curiosity was in full flow and we ended up talking about their experiences for the whole evening. I had learnt by now to be in a 'possibilities' attitude towards this type of discussion, otherwise, I found that if I became judgmental about it, either mentally or emotionally, I would learn nothing and the conversation would inevitably end prematurely. So I stayed in my possibility consciousness – not always easy in the light of our discussion – and explored with these two the claims they wished to make.

They appeared to be enjoying themselves! They recounted all sorts of adventures and in particular they discussed the time they had spent, serving as sort of junior officers on a UFO, and duties they had undertaken on other planets, often far from our solar system. Extraordinary stuff! I didn't really know what to make of it. The only thing I was crystal-clear about was that these two were in complete integrity with themselves. Whoever or whatever they really were, *they totally believed their own story.* This wasn't a con or a play-act. It also seemed to me that they were quite definitely not crazy either. Apart from this revelation, they seemed rather well grounded in the world! So where to from here? I left the Ealing house late that night, wearing an outsize question mark.

The following day however, brought about a shock; a confirmation which had an earth-shattering effect on me! In the late afternoon I went back, unannounced, to the house in Ealing where our visitors were temporarily lodged, to collect some papers. One of the characteristics of the house was that the front door opened absolutely silently; it didn't creak or squeak as the lock was well-oiled and noiseless. The door action was very smooth. So I let myself in and was about to announce myself when I heard Victoria and Jersheirra in the kitchen, laughing and joking light-heartedly about something. They were very close to where I now stood, but out of my line of sight. I am quite certain they could have had no idea that I was there.

I stopped for a moment and eavesdropped shamelessly! Their laughter was centred around a discussion they were having, a little like the fun you might have in recalling the highlights of a recent vacation. As I listened I suddenly stiffened. I heard references to a flight deck...a helmsman...the transition from space to atmosphere...the critical angle of entry when they had arrived on Earth...the buffeting and shake-up this had given the occupants, a rather pompous captain obviously having been caught off guard by it to the stifled amusement of the crew...

'Oh my God', I thought, as it dawned on me that they were laughing about something *which had actually happened while they were serving on board a UFO*, which was apparently travelling to Earth...and they were totally, one hundred per cent sincere. I am quite, quite sure they had no idea I was there at that moment and there they were talking about incidents which had taken place on a UFO. This could not possibly be a scenario that was being played out for my benefit.

I left as quietly as I had come, without announcing myself and deeply shaken. I needed time to think.

Were we really visited by two angels? I cannot, hand on heart, say either 'yes' or 'no' – but, as a genuine possibility, this is a strong contender. I can say, in all sincerity, that if two rather minor angels, as they described themselves, were to incarnate here for a short time to deliver such a message, I can't think of a better or more memorable form for them to appear in than our two 'angels', Jershierra and Victoria!

As you can see, the idea that apparently normal people you may meet can turn out to be very different from what you had assumed, is quite challenging! And yet, these are, perhaps, one of the milder cases. A while later we were to have another adventure that further illustrated this to us:

LEMURIANS

Some months after our two 'angels' had left, we received a phone call from a complete stranger, who identified himself as 'Shield'. He came across as a very pleasant individual, and I warmed to him immediately. He explained that he and his wife Sharula, would shortly be travelling from the USA to Egypt, with a group. They apparently knew Jersheirra and Victoria, who suggested they make contact with us, so could they come and visit us, on their way back from Egypt to the US? And if this was acceptable to us, could we help them to plan some tours in the UK to sites of interest, and perhaps organise the occasional workshop?

We readily agreed. They sounded like interesting people! We did not appreciate just how interesting until they arrived at London's Heathrow Airport, a few weeks later. They had brought quite a crowd with them, as the whole party who had been in Egypt were travelling together. Fortunately, the group split, as some of the entourage were merely changing planes, on their way home. However, we acquired a group of not two but six guests, who were quickly made comfortable in Oonagh's house in the suburb of Ealing.

The following day we introduced ourselves properly. What they told us was fantastic! Sharula, they said, was a princess of royal blood, from present day Lemuria. She came from the city of Telos, *located about a mile below Mount Shasta in Northern California.*

I was to hear a story of not one, but several cities below the Earth's surface. Telos, they told us, is one of a group of underground cities around the planet, all of which are joined by an ultra-fast transportation system – a little like a subway, but operating at around 3,000 miles per hour! The whole network of cities, they said, was known as The Agartha Network.

They explained how this came about. As a result of the fall of Atlantis, the Earth's atmosphere became poisonous for many months. Many of their race perished, but a small group found an extensive natural cave system, in which the air was uncontaminated, and there was plenty of potable water. Using advanced crystal technologies, which in the heyday of Atlantis and Lemuria had stunning implications and powers, they created lighting with a pure sunlight spectrum, and so the underground occupation by a small but determined core group began. A huge engineering task lay ahead of them, but slowly, and with great creativity and effort they developed a multi-level city.

The new colony of Lemurians were totally polarised about one thing: they would not tolerate *any* military functions in their new world. The wars, intellectual and military, that ultimately caused a global catastrophe, represented an unacceptable way of life. Guided by what remained of their priesthood, new values were agreed and promulgated right across the fledgling civilisation. They became what Sharula describes as a temple society. The understanding and integration of spirituality became a primary goal of their education system and the many institutions that developed.

As a result of a focus on spirituality in all aspects of life, the people of this growing underground society began to develop their spiritual faculties. Very soon, there was a marked rise in telepathic ability, and after a few generations, all the New Lemurians were becoming perfect telepaths. They developed protocols between individuals which honoured and respected each individual in such a way that over time, all the natural energetic defences that humans on the Earth's surface put up against each other today had disappeared for these underground people.

Their new and developing way of being, far less brutal in all respects when compared with the behaviour of their above ground cousins (for some had survived there as well), was such that stress was largely eliminated as a New Lemurian experience. This, and their growing use of spiritual faculties that had previously remained latent in most of their society, meant that their life expectancy steadily increased, until it was not unknown to reach an age of 1,000 years! This was explained to me as being much closer to the intended full human life span. The human design intended us to go through four stages of life and not just three, as had previously become normal. Life, developed through all four stages, had not been seen in the surface population for many, many generations.

These four developmental stages were described as:
1) Childhood
2) Adolescence
3) Child bearing
4) The age of wisdom

This last stage began at between 50 and 60 years, at which point a citizen was considered to be fully grown up! In contrast, relatively few humans on the surface ever reached this stage. The current average life expectancy, taken across the planet as a whole, is still under 60 years. Yet for the New Lemurians, this fourth stage represented the vast majority of their lives.

Shield and Sharula told us of present day Lemuria, of their high technologies, very different in both philosophy and content from our own; how the Lemurians are one of the civilisations who operate the spacecraft we know as UFOs (Quazar was to confirm this last fact to us), and many details of their society.

The message which had the greatest impact on us was as follows: *it had been decided in the council of Telos, and endorsed by the other underground cities, that by the turn of the century their civilisation would become totally open to ours, and they would start the process of integrating with the above-ground humans.*

This, they told us, was their purpose. They were here now to start the mission to make those who would listen aware of the existence of an underground civilisation: and of their commitment to join with us, the humanity of the planet's surface.

I was undecided about this fantastic story. It was clear that these people were in integrity with what they told me; in other words, they fully believed it! It was also clear that there were no signs of madness on their part – if you ignored the bizarre nature of their story! Then, about two weeks into their trip, there was a dramatic happening which convinced me of the truth of at least a major part of what I was hearing.

I had seen photographs of Sharula as a beautiful young woman; yet now, only a few years later, she looked very different, as if under great strain, and I would have guessed, perhaps very ill. I had not considered what this might mean. On the night in question, I was sleeping soundly, with our guests presumably doing the same at the Ealing house. I woke at about 4 am, literally shaking with fright (not an usual emotion in my personal repertoire!). I seem to have connected in some way with Sharula's psyche, as if, for a few moments, I actually was her.

My instant understanding was that being brought up as a telepath, she literally lived with her energetic defences completely down all of the time; something that was safe to do if you were a part of a telepathic society which had developed appropriate protocols in their way of being to allow such faculties to develop. However, our society on the planet's surface is quite different. We use our energies like very blunt instruments, lashing out (energetically) frequently, without understanding the barrages of negative energy with which we routinely assail each other.

For an unprotected (in energy terms) telepath, this vicious energy barrage must be absolutely devastating. My early morning connection illustrated to me, in a very personal way, the sacrifice that Sharula was making by committing to an existence on the planet's surface. *She was being so damaged by our brutal use of energies that she was dying, and rapidly.* Somehow, she must have learned how to live with this – after all, being here was a personal commitment that she had made. But while I was briefly connected psychically to her situation, I was deeply shocked and very frightened. I remember Oonagh holding me and comforting me immediately after I awoke – I may have promised her exciting nights, but I'm sure she did not expect this kind of excitement! From my few moments of connection, I also understood that if the story of what Sharula was doing here was, indeed, true, it would have been a conscious sacrifice that only a most loving being would have been able to make!

The other memory I have of that visit, was of another of their group, a young girl (who said she was thirteen years of age) sitting on our lawn talking to about eight people from our own circle of friends. She held the group absolutely spellbound for over an hour as she talked about the energies of the body, specifically of kundalini energy, and what it represents. This is a deeply esoteric subject, and yet here was this young girl, conveying it with a level of knowledge and detail which you might perhaps expect to hear from an aged master after a lifetime's study. I found her level of knowledge and fluency on the subject incredible for a person of her age! And later, as we met more of these people, we realised that there was something very special and unusual about each of them.

What kind of humans would be prepared to risk an almost certain, very premature death, by coming into our society?

We met and worked with Shield and Sharula on several occasions for over three years. We became aware that there was a group around them, who also came from Lemuria. In 1991, I had been taught how to see the aura of any human; that is to say, the energy field that exists around the body. The process for this is essentially one of fine-tuning one's own senses through a quiet and meditative state, and using some energising techniques through deep breathing, so that one's awareness steadily increases. On one occasion, I 'tuned in' to my new friends, and realised that their auras were very much bigger, and different in colour and form, from that of surface humans. I learned to detect the members of their party, eventually identifying around twenty such people.

In 1994 they organised a very large conference in Banff, a town in the Canadian Rocky Mountains, attended by over a thousand delegates. Even though they had never done such a thing before, and the conference lasted for five days with several events happening simultaneously, everything ran perfectly. Oonagh and I attended as guest speakers, had great fun, and were very impressed by the sheer professionalism of the whole operation.

We had several other contacts up to late 1995, and then Shield and Sharula – and all the others around them who we had identified as part of their group – simply disappeared. They left their homes, there was no forwarding address, and none of their friends had any idea where they had gone. I assumed that they have returned from whence they came, to the underground city of Telos. If so, I hope they are recovered from their brush with the energetic brutality of upper Earth. My sense is that they will be back!

Yes, I know that it seems a very tall story! The fact is (as I said before) we always felt that these people were in integrity with what they told us. However crazy it might appear, it was clear they believed and lived their story. They were delightful people; highly developed spiritually and very gentle. And they showed quite remarkable wisdom in all that they did and said.

A third encounter with another type of 'visitor', at the beginning of 1993, was to stretch our belief even further...

ARCTURUS AND THE SPACESHIP

In January 1993 Oonagh and I enjoyed a wonderful trip to Thailand. This came about because she had been visiting a sick relative in Australia over the New Year. At the end of the visit, when Oonagh was about to return to England, she called me up on impulse from Sydney to ask if I would like to meet her 'halfway'. I got out a map and checked; halfway turned out to be Bangkok! What a wonderful treat!

We had some business to take care of in this wonderful, bustling and polluted city, in connection with a group of industrialists who were interested in our Airship project. This kept us there for four days, and then we decided to treat ourselves and visit the Islands. Our choice was a remote, semi-tropical island called Ko Phi Phi, about two hours by boat from the southern mainland, and surrounded by clear, azure waters. It really was a veritable paradise. We stayed in a secluded bay shaded by a canopy of high palm trees, in a small thatched bungalow. We had panoramic views over the beach and the water, and almost total seclusion. The bungalow was part of a discreet hotel complex, memorable for its easy, walk-in atmosphere and wonderful food. What more could we want?

Oonagh had become a very accomplished channel, having been doing this work for over a year. Our 'familiar' entity was Quazar, a galactic energy being with whom we set up specific procedural protocols, and who taught us how to protect ourselves energetically while we were using this form of communication. One evening, after a particularly relaxed and happy day, we decided to do some channelling work.

We went through our usual procedures at some length and connected with Quazar. We had a fairly normal discussion – we can't remember the content of this – and there was nothing out of the ordinary, until we arrived at a point where I detected a subtle change in the nuance of the energy and in the tonality of the voice. We had been primed by Quazar about making our challenges if there was any doubt as to who Oonagh was channelling. I decided that this would be an appropriate moment to challenge. "Who am I speaking with?" I asked.

"You are speaking with Arcturus," came the response. I was taken aback since we were not used to other beings 'gate-crashing' our channelling sessions in this way, and this was an entity we had not previously encountered and so we knew nothing about him! Remembering what we had been taught by Quazar, I went through the usual challenges and the responses were quite in order so all seemed to be well. I then engaged Arcturus in conversation. He told me that he had come to teach me how to recognise, and work with, certain kinds of energies. We had a somewhat schoolroom-like session; I was definitely in a learning situation, which was extremely interesting but is really not a relevant part of this story. Eventually, we ended the channelling and re-focused on enjoying the island.

We continued with our wonderful holiday and after a few days flew back to London browned and rested, and decidedly the better for our break. The second night after our return home we decided to do some channelling once again...

I went through the familiar routine, clearing and cleansing the space, and calling in Quazar and the other entities we had met through him to support us in our task and then, as Oonagh started to channel, I conducted a series of challenges to make sure that we were dealing with the right entity, just as we had been taught. However, when I came to the point where I asked "Who am I speaking with...?" a voice replied "This is Arcturus..."

Now this had definitely NEVER happened before. The protocol we had arranged was that Quazar would always, always be with us first and would be present while we spoke with any other being. This safeguarded us against the risk of being 'invaded' by less desirable beings and was an unvarying procedure which we had agreed with Quazar, and we regarded it as something of an absolute. Now, here we were dealing with Arcturus whom we had only met once before and who had commenced the session by summarily breaking our protocol. I didn't know what to think!

"Arcturus," I said, "you know we have a protocol in these matters. Why have you broken it?"

"Well," said Arcturus, "in your terms Quazar is many, many millions of miles away from you and we have to relay his energy to bring him to you. I, on the other hand, am very close to you in your physical terms at this moment. It therefore seemed pointless to project myself to what you would understand to be a remote point, in the circumstances."

We discussed this for a few moments. The explanation seemed perfectly adequate and reasonable, and we went on with the business of the evening.

Now we have a friend called John Frank who is mentioned quite a few times in these stories, and who is a very capable clairvoyant. Over the years, we had worked with him on many, many occasions and our relationship has always been close. At the time of this story, we hadn't spoken to John for perhaps six weeks as we had been both busy and latterly, away. John was about to enter the scene with information that was to prove quite electrifying!

The morning after the Arcturus channelling, John rang me, his voice full of suppressed excitement at 8 am; the hour itself being most unusual.

"Peter," he said, sounding definitely flustered. "My committee have some information which they wish me to relay to you."

John works through a committee of five energy beings who are in a different dimension to the rest of us, and who are very wise and, on occasion, quite playful. This call was odd for despite the fact that John had established contact with me, he appeared reluctant to go ahead with what he had to say. After a slightly circular discussion which was leading us nowhere, I pressed him to get on with it (well, patience has never been my strongest point and it was very early in the morning!) and he responded by saying slowly, "Peter, this is going to sound really off the wall!"

"John," I retorted, trying my best to be patient, "much of what we do is really off the wall. You of all people should be used to that by now..."

"No, no," said John, "this is *really* off the wall." This kind of exchange went on for a bit. I felt my patience evaporating to the point of exasperation.

"Come on, John, just what is this message?"

Reluctantly, John said, "Well, I have my committee on the line," (meaning that he was communicating with them at the same time as he was communicating with me), "and they wish you to know that there is a mother ship on permanent station above your houseboat..."

"What!" I exclaimed, my disbelief system was already kicking into gear.

There was a short pause while John communicated with the committee. "Well, it's a very large space vessel in a shifted dimension. And it is on permanent station working in some way with the energies of the planet."

"Oh, really," I asked sceptically and a little sarcastically, "and just how big is this thing?" This was beginning to seem extremely unreal. Was I dreaming this entire conversation?

"Well," John said hesitantly, "they tell me that it stretches from Hampton Court to Richmond."

"Wow!" I thought. This made it a behemoth, a vast structure some seven or eight miles long. I put this to John.

"Yes," he exclaimed, "this is just what they mean."

I asked how many souls or entities were on board.

"In excess of ten thousand," the committee relayed to me via John. I tried to focus my reeling mind sufficiently to ask about prosaic things like the shape of the vessel and the number of decks.

"Well," they told me, again through John, "it exists through a number of dimensions. It is not really a form that we can describe to you adequately."

The discussion went on and on. I learnt something of interest, but many of my more obvious questions clearly couldn't be answered within my three-dimensionally oriented understanding. My disbelief continued to rise until it was almost total.

"Well," I finally exclaimed, metaphorically throwing up my hands in total exasperation. "And just who is in command of this ship?"

John replied a bit defensively, "I have no idea. Hold on a minute, I'll ask the committee..."

John was off the line for about 30 seconds. When he came back to me he was somewhat perplexed. "I have received," he said, "the most peculiar answer – I'm not sure I've got this right – they say that you have been in contact with him over the last few hours!"

"Yes, yes," I said, getting distinctly annoyed, "but just WHO is this being?"

"His name," John said slowly, "is ARCTURUS..."

I simultaneously dropped the telephone, and fell off the stool I was sitting on. It slowly began to sink in. It was an indisputable fact that I had never talked to John about anything or anyone called Arcturus; or any name even remotely like it. This was a completely new name in our conversation as far as he was concerned. Oonagh and I had only spoken to Arcturus for the first time ourselves a few days earlier through our initial channelling in Ko Phi Phi.

Perhaps this was just one of those little synchronicities to show that however wild an idea may appear on the surface, there is a fair chance it is true?

This story also has a 'sting in the tail'. Though we subsequently channelled Arcturus quite a few times, we had no real idea as to who he might be. In the course of our conversations, at our request, he described himself. He told us that he was a little like an Ascended Master, not from Earth, but from the Arcturian star system, and in our terms, a very long while back.

As described in Chapter 9, and about eighteen months after the first encounter with Arcturus, we visited some friends in Somerset on New Year's Day. One of them gave me a book called *The Seven Mighty Elohim*, with a chapter on each of these beings, referred to in the Bible, and who are believed in esoteric circles to be the actual builders of the Universe – those entities who take the divine plan and express it in the physical dimension.

You might imagine the impact it had on me, when I opened the seventh chapter, to find that the seventh of the Elohim profiled was...ARCTURUS !

About three months after this incident, we were to have another surprise from Arcturus: and evidence that yet another type of visitor may be amongst us!

BIRDMEN

During a channelling session, we asked questions about the functions of these great 'mother ships' we were told about. It emerged that a primary task for them is to observe and monitor the progress of humanity. My natural curiosity prompted me to ask Arcturus how they went about this.

An important point here is that *Velma* where our session took place has a wooden roof. It means that rain and occasionally, birds or animals on the roof create very distinctive sound effects for those within.

Arcturus explained that Galactic conventions governing their actions do not allow them to make their presence known in the physical sense. They are subject to what the TV series Star Trek calls *'the Prime Directive'*. They are not allowed to interfere with our development. He stated that many of the beings on board the ships are humanoid, essentially like us, but because they exist in a less dense environment than us they possess certain additional faculties. He referred specifically to the ability to project themselves into our dimension in some convenient form that would not be seen by us as anything out of the ordinary.

"Our normal operating mode," he said, "is to send observers down to the planet's surface in the form of birds. In this form, we can observe all that we wish without causing the slightest consternation". We discussed the details of this amazing claim for a few moments, and then he offered, "Would you like a demonstration?"

Naturally, we assured him that yes, we would very much like a demonstration! A split second later we heard the sounds of a large bird landing on the roof above us, taking several scrabbled steps which suggested that it was not wholly out of the air, and then the flapping of wings as this brief visit turned back into take off, and flight. We then saw a large crow fly away from us into the distance. The whole event had been so instantaneous, immediately we had assented to the demonstration, that there could be little doubt in our minds – and this session was recorded on tape, which still illustrates the impact of those bird noises very well!

We were all surprised, somewhat shocked, and quite elated by this illustration that, yet again, all may well not be as it seems!

So, are we being visited and observed in this way? It would certainly be convenient and safe for all parties. I shall never again watch the abundant bird-life around me with quite the same detachment as I had shown prior to this incident!

So the overall message is quite clear to me: nobody around us is necessarily what they seem!

VISITORS

Each sheaf of grass
    adds
Its own drop of dew
    to wash
The passing traveller's feet
    just
As our desert-fathers
Used to do
For strangers passing through:

What gladdening event
    to have the new
Enter
Our so familiar tent!

Chapter Thirteen

Integration And Metamorphosis

INTEGRATION

The Era of Exploring
      what each is
           on its own
      is clearly
At an end:
      now we must learn
To blend our 'different-nesses' once again!

If we by now
      have not begun to see
Our meaning,
      value lies
But in Community
      of everything
           of all there is,
The pains of differentiating
      separating out,
           dissecting
Will have been all in vain,
      and we'll have missed
The whole point of life's exercise.

The 'game' of separation – for that is how, earlier in this book, we elected to see it – has been an integral part of our human journey and an essential component of the Fall. The great task that humanity has as it ascends, includes the reversal of this game of separation, which we have all played for hundreds of generations. Here is a channelled communication from Shilam Si Ra on just what this means. In the first chapter he described how souls split into many parts, in order that more experiences could be gained, more quickly. Here, he talks about the reverse process:

Great commitment to the Light, or God, within you, usually means that great darkness also awaits integration, and for some of you, your group soul is recollecting, re-member-ing itself, for the ascent, the move back up the frequencies that is the reversal of 'The Fall'. No one knew how difficult the acceptance of the soul's various parts would be when the game began. Only now, in the time when a batch of human souls is about to complete their journey, are we being confronted with our greatest darkness which has learned all the dark lessons for us. No one guessed how much judgement and distance would result from this process and that some souls would not want to take back their opposites when it came time to re-member.

Note that here the term 're-member' is being used as the opposite to 'dis-member'. To continue:

This is what we are being presented with – our own soul's darkness – each of us facing whatever wholeness means, when we reclaim all of our pieces. All of us who choose to accept this journey as our reality come face-to-face with darkness that equals all the light within us. It takes great courage to face that and honour the part of our self that experienced the worst, most horrible and darkest night of the soul. Great fear may come up because the one you are in this limited existence cannot comprehend the magnitude of the experiences of the 'others'. It is not unlike honouring soldiers who fought the battles which were imposed on them by those who would not fight themselves.

Judgement day is here for many of us, and we are our own judges; our 'life review' comes up, and it is not just one life, but all the lives lived by all our pieces, coming to consciousness for final review to see if all the lessons of this earth existence have been learned. If they have, we have but to complete etheric life which is the first level of ascension – mastery over matter. Coming and going at will without getting caught in the density of matter again is what it is about, then this game is over. Begin anew on another course of choice."

Although the concept of 'Judgement day' has long been used as a device to frighten and control, I believe that this is most inappropriate. I see it in another way. For me it is a little like riding a great surfing wave. You can choose to get on to the front of the wave, and have a truly exhilarating ride. Of course, there will be moments of fright, when you doubt you ability to stay on. You may even fall off, and have to catch the next wave! But the only danger lies in complete inflexibility. The only ones in any real danger are those who stand, unyielding at the water's edge as hundreds of tons of water bear down on them, fists raised in defiance and shouting 'No Way!'

The accelerating changes around us are like that wave; with flexibility of mind and intent, we will enjoy the ride, even if at times it feels more than a little crazy at times!

We can take this 'wave' analogy a little further. It has often been stated in recent esoteric writings that there will be three waves of ascension; that the opportunity will be repeated three times. Eventually, only a very small percentage of the global population, if any at all, will hold out and remain totally rigid, as they see what is going on around them. So a key message is: **Be flexible, explore what is happening – and don't worry about it!**

In one of our discussions with Quazar, we looked at the effect of the twenty-one comet fragments that had then hit Jupiter; which event seems to have been the trigger point for much of the accelerating change that has happened since. The energy of this great collision appears to be part of the 'waking up' process for the planet and humanity. It has also triggered the issue about integrating the light and the dark. This channelled conversation took place on the 15th August 1994. Also present are Ken and Benedicta.

Peter: *Quazar, much has been happening over the last week and in particular the series of collisions with Jupiter have now finished, at least in their physical sense. I would be very grateful if you could review for us what the effect of this has been and what we might now expect as a result.*

Quazar: *This has been like a massive thunderbolt would be, hitting you, striking to the very core of your being. It has created much tension in the universe because Jupiter is a massive body that gives out strong energies across the solar system, which is itself now resonating with Jupiter's energies. We are working together now to keep those energies diverted as much as possible from the earth, and some of these energies will benefit the earth but not of course to the extent that they reverberate across the universe.*

Peter: *So a full measure of these energies would be damaging to us?*

Quazar:	*This is how we interpret it.*
Peter:	*Are these energies still building up or have they reached their peak?*
Quazar:	*They have much build-up to go.*
Peter:	*And so do you have any understanding of how we might experience this?*
Quazar:	*You are already experiencing it. In the roller coaster of your feelings, your emotions, your relationships, the tensions, the explosiveness; like thunderbolts of actions by others and their impacts upon you.*
Peter:	*It sounds as though we are in for a fairly bumpy ride if this has far from peaked as yet.*
Quazar:	*This is not necessarily a bumpy ride. These energies are actually beneficial. Think of the energy put in a beaker of liquid to separate out the solids from the liquids. If you will, this process is a similar one of separating out the light workers (we use that term advisedly) from those who will not move on for now.*
Peter:	*Thank you.*
Quazar:	*You have called it polarisation. You might call it precipitation: separation is a term we understand you choose not to use, because you desire to create one world, one planet, one united consciousness in mental, physical, emotional and spiritual consciousness. This is an admirable, laudable seeking, yet it is time you recognise that perhaps it may not be for the full consciousness to move together in the future. You have indeed moved as one consciousness over these past years since the visitation of the Christ energy.*
Peter:	*Are we talking of this being what our Bible calls Judgement Day, which is a separation?*

Quazar: *This metaphor has been so misinterpreted in your consciousness that it is not such a healthy metaphor to use. The judging of the quick and the dead is not so helpful a concept at this time!*

Peter: *But in some form it means a separation of humanity as the next step is taken.*

Quazar: *Yes, and there is danger of course, in this conversation. The danger of those who believe themselves to be in the light moving rapidly into the dark through ego and believing themselves to somehow be better. None of God's children are better or worse than any others. There is no stigma, failure, disadvantage for those who choose to stay at certain aspects of evolutionary consciousness.*

Peter: *So this is a choice each of us will make somewhere in our consciousness?*

Quazar: *And there is no right or wrong choice...*

Peter: *I think so Quazar. Yes.*

Quazar: *Perhaps one of you would feed back to me your understanding and we can explore this further?*

Peter: *Well, Quazar, I think everybody is stunned.*

Quazar: *This is my sense. Perhaps I am not communicating with each of you as clearly as would be helpful. Perhaps each of you would for me communicate what you are hearing, and what your feeling about that is? Perhaps also your experience of the "Judgement Day" metaphor?*

Benedicta: *It's hard to put into words, Quazar, but I will try. You're saying that the Jupiter energy is helping mass consciousness to precipitate at the moment? And that people will find their own levels, and that wherever that level is, people will be most comfortable in it, so it's the element of being in the right place rather than an actual judgement which is important. Wherever people are, the circumstances will be appropriate for them. Is that correct?*

Quazar: *Thank you Benedicta, you express it so well.*

Benedicta: *Is there anything that can be done to help that precipitation? So that if there are any lingering doubts, shall we say fate is not decided in terms of doubts and that all can be cleared?*

Quazar: *It is happening. the most powerful role each can play is first to be unconditionally loving of the self, honouring what is true for the self and honouring others for what is true for them. The highest is not necessarily the best. It is the level which is best for you which is 'the best'. So you can be as you find yourself. In your life you wish to be among like-minded souls, like-minded spirits who are in the same level of experience-conscious evolution as you are. You would not be so happy were you with those more highly or less consciously evolved.*

Ken: *So what you were saying about judgement day is that most of us that come here have made the choices about our lives before we came, and others have chosen to be where they are also. Would that be correct?*

Quazar: *You choose to come into this world in a certain situation and your work is always the evolution of the consciousness you carry; the growing into the light. Each lifetime you move more or less closer to the light. This is a path which the soul enters onto in carnation.*

Ken: *How would that affect someone who was having their first incarnation on this planet?*

Quazar: *If we are speaking of those who we have called the true light workers – those who have come for one incarnation only for the purpose of supporting unconditionally, lovingly supporting this phase of earth's evolution, then they will automatically be separated and will return to their homes once their job here is completed.*

Ken: *Would that apply to anyone in this group?*

Quazar: *No! This is not so here. You are all evolved human beings with previous incarnations on this planet. Each of you working through the conscious evolution of your spirit.*

At any time everyone is of course divinely loved wherever they are and whichever way they choose to move. From the cosmic viewpoint there is no right or wrong. A soul may take many lifetimes moving backwards, in your terms away from the light, only to leap forward in another lifetime as a result, if you will, of overcoming the Karma of previous lifetimes. It is not a path from A to B step by step, no ups no downs, at the same rate, each soul compared to each soul. Every soul on this planet has free will to move up, down, wherever they wish at whatever speed they wish – and wherever they are is perfect.

If we are not to be judged on our relative performance – a great relief for many – just what is the key task required in the matter of ascension back up the frequencies? And if some kind of 'Judgement Day' is a factor in getting started, what form might it take? Quazar spoke about this on a second occasion, on 13th December 1995, giving us rather more insight into the processes involved:

Peter: *We have had a number of contacts amongst our group – telepathic and channelled contacts and physical sensations – connecting us with various of the space fleets that are here. We get the impression that these beings, while they are not opposed to us, have agendas that they would like to offer or impose on humanity. We see it as very important that humanity should develop its own agenda. Could you comment please?*

Quazar: *This is, of course, just another agenda! It is time, as humanity now goes through this rapid change, for many human beings to face their own god, to face the inner god within them and the God that is all-that-is, and that connects all consciousness. This is the moment of judgement day, that you have had written in your books, your bibles, your teachings. This is the time you now face, and it is for humanity to come to its own deliverance, its own truth, its own deep and wise understanding, one by one, individual by individual, of divinity and truth.*

Peter: *So, you are saying that this can only be an inner-directed process, of and for the individual?*

Quazar: *Indeed, and for many it may not be like that; no-one can prescribe. Each individual will be moved in their own way, to find their own truth. It will not be possible to judge anyone else except yourself. One person will find their own truth is to participate in an organised religion, as you might perceive it. That doesn't make them any more or less likely to be in alignment with God, all-that-is. Another may deny all spiritual awareness, apparently have none, and yet be completely aligned with God, all-that-is. Many who are apparently godless will be totally at one with God, and others who are apparently so good and such great light workers will be totally unaligned with God, all-that-is. All you may do, each one of you, is be true to your own inner connection, your own inner God, all-that-is.*

Human consciousness has now moved exponentially through its growth in ways which we had never anticipated, and nor had you! So, we now see that these 'judgement days' of which we speak, may come much quicker for many human beings, and they will find that their release from this place, if that is what they choose, will be quicker than it might have been.

You see, for some souls, this is not 'heaven on Earth'. Others, they can experience the heaven that is the earth, but some who are less...maybe developed, maybe experienced and maybe just not wishing to be here, belonging elsewhere; they are released. There are many different types of souls present, there are some who are not here as human beings at all; they are only visiting in human form to complete a task, and when that task is completed, it is for them to choose whether to be here any more, or not.

So, it appears that humanity is in for a long period of testing, where we will hold ourselves up to the standards of our own higher selves, and compare ourselves against them. What happens to us as soul beings after that will depend, in great measure, on this 'self assessment'.

One major area where we will be challenged is our understanding of 'Good and Evil', and what we are expected to do about it in the context of integration. As far as is possible, I would like to present an all-round view of the whole issue of integrating light and dark. In order to look at this process from another viewpoint, I shall examine the implications of the 'Dark Angel' Asphondel, the one who turned up as a major player, facilitating a miraculous healing in *The Philip Story*. He appears, to the small group who have experienced him, as a being of high purpose and integrity. Yet he could also be characterised by those who are polarised and inflexible as 'an instrument of the devil' (the stuff of excommunication etc). There is clearly a mystery here, and it seems valuable to express what he may mean to us, thus putting this 'Good/Evil', 'Light/Dark' quandary into perspective.

In our private Internet group we started a great debate on the subject towards the end of 1995, stirring up something of a hornets' nest. The reason for this will become clear as this chapter progresses. It is a very relevant subject and it is not easy to deal with for many, many, apparently enlightened people!

For aeons, humanity has been 'doing separation'; highlighting and exploiting differences between cultures, tribes, nations, political viewpoints etc. As stated in my Introduction, these differences are manipulated by monarchs, dictators, politicians and religions all over the world to create political power. If you create a 'them', and convince your group that 'they' are a major threat, then you have control, by having taken power from the group – being empowered by them! But such power is always at the expense of whoever is characterised as 'them', who are now branded negatively in the minds of 'us'. Of course, those ambitious for control also exist on the 'them' side, and play the same game in reverse.

Are we willing to give up this 'them and us' scenario? We can choose instead to celebrate the great diversity of peoples on Earth, leading each individual who makes this choice into a totally different mind-set on the whole global situation, and the options for improving it. Separation lies at the root of many difficult international situations, and the solutions are critically dependent on the ending of separation. World peace and harmony is what integration is all about! It is a great coming together, a conjoining of all aspects and all peoples.

Over the years, I have had the privilege of travelling to many remote places, and I am quite certain that the very best adventures are to be had while one is within other peoples' cultures; but only if one is truly 'open' to the experience. Some of the most effective learning situations come about when you sit and talk with people from a quite different background! A simple, pro-active question you can ask yourself is: 'How many of my friends are from different cultures, political backgrounds, religions, skin colours?' If the answer is 'very few' then I suggest that in the name of integration and positive change on the planet, you may have some serious work to do!

There is another crucial challenge we have to address. We cannot stand for integration and simultaneously hold a fixed vision of 'evil'; the deepest essence of separation. The issue is perhaps our biggest challenge, and needs to be handled with both circumspection, and a degree of intrepidity. This is an area where the dictum 'fools rush in where angels fear to tread' is self-evidently true. So I shall go slowly, and endeavour *not* to be a fool in this particular matter! Let me give you a brief history in story form of experiences that have led me to certain key conclusions:

A LESSON IN GLASTONBURY

Three times in recent years I have been 'summoned' to Glastonbury by people I did not know – and each

such summons turned out to be the start of a new adventure! The occasion of this story was in the autumn of 1993. An American woman acquaintance phoned me to say that she was in the UK and filming near Glastonbury. She had a day free before she flew out, so I agreed to drive there to meet her...

I have a friend, Mary Tara (See *The Glastonbury Vortex* in Chapter 8) who lives at the healing centre called Shamballah on the lower slopes of Glastonbury Tor. That morning I arrived in Glastonbury early, and decided that I would call on her, and beg a greeting hug and an early morning cup of tea before going on to my meeting. However, the upshot of my 'brief' visit was that there was so much going on at Shamballah, and such a lot of news to exchange, that I called the American lady and said 'come on over', which she did!

We all got down to some serious talking, as other people arrived, quite unplanned, including another American, John. Very soon there were six of us sitting in a circle in a secluded cottage in the grounds, talking about spiritual events, and how they were affecting our lives. Yet again in my life, another powerful group had come together with no planning whatsoever – at least, not on the physical plane! I instinctively knew that there was some reason, perhaps some new lesson, to be learned here.

It was a most stimulating gathering, and we all enjoyed the interchange. Someone said "I know we all have a sense of our individual purpose in being here, and I would like to suggest that we all say who we really are, and what our purpose on the planet is at this time." Lofty stuff! We moved the discussion in this direction when, quite suddenly, there was a change of atmosphere as John, sounding somewhat distressed, broke in. He said, most urgently, "Look, I'm afraid that if I tell you who I believe I am, and my background, you may well not want me to be here..."

The group was naturally inquisitive! We all wanted to know who John might be, and whatever credentials were worrying him, immediately!

He told us, somewhat haltingly at first, that he was aware that for many previous incarnations he had been 'not of the light'. Indeed, he felt he had been some kind of emissary for the dark forces, although he also sincerely felt this did not apply to his current life. He told us that he believed he had come into this life to deliver a specific message. We were riveted to hear what was to come next. What he had to say was as follows:

"Our physical universe has, for aeons, moved cyclically, from dominance by the light to the dark and back to the light, an endless sequence of one coming into supremacy, followed by the other. Light to dark to light to dark over thousands of centuries, affecting not only the physical plane, but many other planes of consciousness."

Yes, we all understood so far! I wondered just where this revelation was taking us. There was a few minutes of discussion at this point as the members of the party focused on the subject matter. John waited patiently for silence, and when he had everyone's undivided attention once more, he went on:

"Now, the time is approaching when something quite new can emerge – the arrival of the Christ energy, which will start to happen soon. When it comes into play, it means that there are no longer just two primary forces at work (these being what we choose to call 'good' and 'evil') but that they are now being joined by a third".

Again, we discussed what he meant. It emerged that the energy he was talking about was, in some way, to be an integrated energy that contained both some aspects of light and dark, and in addition, a cohesiveness that would beneficially affect everything in our physical world soon. To continue with John:

"This means that the age-old cycle of alternating light and dark can potentially end, because three forces acting together form a triad, which is stable, rather than a duality; therefore the cycling between light and dark will stop. This is a unique opportunity, which will change many things for the better, not just on Earth, but throughout the Cosmos. It is most rare for anything genuinely new to happen in the Universe. It is so vast, and so old in our terms, that literally everything we might see as unique has been tried somewhere before. Yet the emergence of the Christ energy in this way is quite new – nothing like this has ever happened in the experience of the whole of this universe before."

John went on to say that this would be a great challenge for humanity, perhaps its greatest task yet, and paradoxically, those individuals who saw themselves as being 'enlightened' i.e. 'of the light' (by the then current paradigm), would face their greatest individual challenge.

I was shocked; we all were. We even managed a short period of complete silence! This was the very first occasion when this possibility of an end to 'good and evil' had been made clear to me. John's revelation about himself did not mean he was ejected from the gathering; far from it. What he said became the focal point for a whole day's vigorous discussion, and took all of us into a new, and challenging understanding of one of the great changes we are to see in our lifetimes!

Over the next few days I started to integrate this information. As I did so, my understanding underwent a radical expansion. I realised that the fundamental concept of 'Light and Dark' was a natural part of the universe that we are manifest in – without it, there would be no contrast. None of the subtleties, none of the 'shadings' we experience would be available. This applies not just in the visual sense, but also in the energy sense.

More importantly, in the energy sense it became apparent to me that we were a part of a perfectly balanced energy system. There was an exact amount of light to balance the dark at every level of existence. It was clear to me that we, and all around us, had been created by the very phenomenon of separation. This meant there was a further problem: human beings of high intent had, for hundreds of generations, been calling for 'more light, more light' in their prayers, hymns, invocations and incantations. If it were true that we are part of a highly inter-linked and perfectly balanced energy continuum, then this apparently laudable call could only result in one thing – *an equal amount of 'more dark', would appear somewhere else.*

In calling for 'more light' through millions of human beings subscribing to many different religions, we had collectively failed to note one vital fact: even in the darkest of times, human beings, especially when operating in large groups, have always had the power to manifest. What this constant supplication did, over long periods of time, was to polarise the natural concept of 'light and dark' (without which we could not exist) to the far more radical position of 'Good and Evil'. We, humanity, had literally invented, and given great energy to this thing called 'Evil' by further polarizing what had existed naturally all along.

So a chance decision to 'drop in for a cup of tea' had led me through a great adventure in understanding – my world had been permanently expanded as a result!

After my encounter at Shamballah, several pieces of the jigsaw emerged by way of further knowledge which illustrated the 'light/dark' balancing process, and the potential for imbalance. The first concerned the role of the Essenes. The book *Two Thirds* (referred to in Chapter 7) interestingly portrays a mysterious group known as the Essenes as having evolved from star travellers who came here from a distant galaxy. They were the hidden guides and caretakers for other advanced civilisations, since before life on Earth, and they have always been 'where the action is' in terms of the development of sentient life!

Shortly after my first realisation about the difficulty caused by the polarisation of light and dark, I attended a lecture which focused mainly on the story of how the Essenes had been responsible for much of Christ's spiritual education as a young man. The overall effect of their strict and painstaking religious discipline, over many generations, was that they succeeded in taking 'the light' to a whole new level in the centuries before Christ. They were thus an important factor in the creation of a matching energy of dark elsewhere on the planet, and were instrumental in moving separation to another level! This may of course have been the object of the exercise, in order that humanity could learn the lessons of separation! You may recall that in my introduction to this book I concluded that our planet has 'turmoil' built into it – precisely so that we can learn!

This is not the only time such a thing has happened. Consider as another example, the case of the Buddha. According to legend, when the Buddha attained enlightenment, he took a truly huge step forward, in the process of which he released a great deal of 'light' energy. The difficulty was that it could not be integrated into the planet, for neither humanity, nor the earth spirit (known to many as Gaia, the 'earth mother') were ready for it.

Legend has it that Buddha was eventually slain by a demon bandit called 'Anguli Mala'; the name translates literally as 'necklace of fingers'. The energy being behind Anguli Mala is said to have been the Angel of Restraint, which performed a necessary task in the context of the human experiment. In modern parlance, the Buddha was 'taken out': the implication being that humanity was not sufficiently far along its journey of development to integrate this great Buddha energy. If this had not been done, then arguably the effect may have been that a great matching energy of 'dark' would have developed, in order to re-balance the total energy system on the planet!

At a gathering in 1994, the practicalities of this understanding was illustrated to us quite forcefully! Here is the story of what happened:

LIGHT AND DARK AT RAVEN'S AIT

Raven's Ait is an island in the river Thames, at Kingston, a few miles above London. Of course the Raven is, in many cultures, regarded as a messenger of the dark forces! But others, American Indian tribes, for example, see their presence as a good luck sign!

It all began in 1994. Oonagh and I went on a springtime trip to Canada as guest speakers (on the subject of 'Global Change and the mechanisms for recognising and supporting change processes') at a wonderful conference called the Conclave of Michael. In one of the sessions which we facilitated, encouraging participants to take a leadership position in their lives and beliefs, a young woman, Sharon, stood up and spoke with eloquence and passion about her vision. We subsequently talked with her for a while after the end of the meeting, and encouraged her to take a leadership role in expressing what she had envisaged.

Some weeks later, we had a phone call from her. She was calling from her home in Vancouver and explained that she wanted to hold a gathering in London, within four weeks. In the meantime, there were to be several conference calls in which the potential participants would be briefed as to what was going on.

Sharon had experienced a series of powerful visions over a period of three to four years, in which she saw that a new energy was to penetrate the energy system of the planet, and bring about huge and positive changes. I should explain that it is a widely held belief that things happen at an energetic level first, and are later translated into physical 'reality'. The image that Sharon was given for the penetration of this energy was 'the beak of the Dove'. As the dove is an almost universal symbol for peace, nobody had any difficulty with this concept, although there was a huge amount of information about how this energy might be facilitated.

Our response to Sharon's call was that we would be delighted to be a part of the group, just as long as we did not end up organising everything!

Dates were set, and a few days before the event, people flew in from all over the world: the US, Canada, Hawaii, Japan, and arrived at our houseboat, looking for somewhere to sleep! We soon realised that our accommodation was running out fast, and that my original concern was correct, there were no arrangements in place for the conference itself, or for housing any of the attendees.

I decided to ring round suitable venues, a very difficult task in early summer at zero notice! My first call was to Raven's Ait, an island where there was a conference centre attached to a sail training establishment for young people. I had used the island before for the occasional business conference, and knew that it had sleeping facilities for up to 60 people, so that as we were to be about two dozen in total, it could be ideal. I also knew that it was usually booked solid all the way through the summer!

I rang. They confirmed my worst fears. 'We are booked out until September,' and then added 'apart from this next week, which is free'! Problem solved! We made arrangements, shipped everyone to the island, settled in and got underway! It was a great gathering, with mystics, healers, lawyers, architects, ex-navy and army officers and business people, all of different ethnic and cultural origins, mixing freely, and with respect for each other's viewpoints. We covered much ground, but while we were on Raven's Ait, there was a series of strange happenings.

At that time, our channelling had started to focus our attention on the desirability and real implications of integration. We were asked, some time earlier, to change our invocations, the non-religious prayers we always did at gatherings to ask for support from other realms. We were asked to invoke the light (as we had always done), and then invite 'those that we had consigned to darkness, who were willing to work with us in good faith, to come forth and co-create with the light'. This was a first move towards integration, but it seemed outrageous at the time; consequently, feeling that we were treading on glass, we did little about it!

On the third day at Raven's Ait, I did a private meditation with Sharon. We retreated to Richmond Park (very beautiful at this time of the year, or indeed, at any time), to have a heart-to-heart about what was going on. We faced up to the fact that after three days, despite a promising start, the whole group was dead-ended, with a fair amount of disagreement in full swing! As we sat, a very clear voice in my head reminded me of the request for the 'new-style' invocation. It said 'we hold the barriers that humanity has manifested. If you wish us to co-create with the light, we can assist you in navigating around them, but we need you to ask for our help'.

We noted this, and decided to take the lead. The following morning the whole group had a serious debate on the subject of 'light and dark' integration. For some, it was initially very challenging. Eventually after much passing of the talking stick (a traditional American Indian way to ensure that all have their say in a group), we decided that, with proper protection, we should take this vital step towards integration.

It is a basic principle that when anyone says a prayer (regardless of their religious beliefs) they are inevitably addressing the forces of 'the light'. Indeed, any prayer to forces of the dark would be regarded as some form of black magic, which I would personally stay well away from. However, here, we were being asked to invoke both light and dark forces, to work together in supporting our invocation by co-creating.

One of our number was John Tozeland, a Canadian Indian shaman, very capable with things of the spirit. He led this first invocation including the co-creation words we were given. The energy generated was fantastic – very positive. We all felt that this was a purposeful development, but with a need for safeguards, which we inserted into the whole process. The effect was to release what seemed to be a whirlwind of positive energy; not a frightening experience, but a very joyful one. As a result, the whole group was un-blocked, and everything progressed smoothly and quickly.

The next astonishing move, followed that night in the most unexpected way!

Sometimes I get severe gout, always in my right foot; unimaginably painful, and fortunately not very often. I have been affected by it once or twice every year, for about twenty years. When I have an attack, it takes several hours to get going, during which time I am aware of an impending attack and can do something about it. Modern pills, taken in good time, can remove it quite rapidly. If I miss this opportunity, and it gets hold, I know I will be in pain for up to three days.

I woke at about 4.00 am, in such pain (apparently from a gout attack) that I woke Oonagh and told her I felt suicidal – something I have never in my life said before. There was no warning of the attack, and none of the usual build-up. Oonagh has good healing energy, so she assisted by using her hands over my foot, under the bedcovers, to reduce the pain.

After a few moments she said, rather tentatively, "This is going to sound silly, but there is a being present here..." She described a black hooded figure, who was laughing at her, but not unkindly. She concentrated on this figure and he spoke to her, saying "You have invited us here to co-create, and now you must deal with me." She was most taken aback as she relayed what she was seeing and hearing. I am far more robust with the Hermes energy as a major part of my energetic make-up, than Oonagh with her 'fairy' energy, so I called on the being to address me directly, which he did, communicating with me telepathically.

The first thing he said was "I am going to release you from the pain in your foot, and there are no conditions for doing this...!"

I had been told when working with my friend Rajan Samra in a guided meditation, that at the very earliest times of humanity on the Earth, the being Hermes had been "nailed to the Earth, so that he could not fly – by his right foot". Apparently, this was done to keep his energy available to humanity and the planet as they went through their long journey; for quite what purpose, I am never really sure. In some way, my gout seemed to be a reflection of this past assault carried in this 'Hermetic' energy!

The being now addressing me said it was he who had originally done this, and he was releasing me. Within minutes the pain had gone. On any other occasion, if the gout had got to this state, full relief would have taken days; and I have not had gout since! The being turned out to be the dark angel Asphondel, with whom we had contact on many other future occasions.

He said, "You have been calling on us to co-create, and we wish to join you and work together in good faith. But there is a problem, and I have a request of you..." He explained that these beings were subject to Karma, a build-up of negative (in this case) energy from past acts that required re-balancing, and that they were carrying a great karmic burden. His request was that the group at Raven's Ait should come together in the morning, and debate the experience I had gone through. If we could agree, *Asphondel requested that we carry out a meditation of forgiveness for the dark angelic forces.* This would enable them to join with those of the light in the future, in order that all could work together, to co-create.

We did what was requested, having talked it over very seriously first, and conducted a remarkable series of meditations and prayers, forgiving those of the dark forces who wished, in good faith, to bring an end to separation and co-create a new beginning. The energies around this were quite incredible: there was the greatest sense of cosmic partying I have ever experienced, and I believe it was quite real and genuine. It had appeared like a great risk, literally a shot in the dark, as we went through the experience, but the result seemed unambiguously successful!

We finished our work: the group generated a strategy for a global change program that could be adopted by many groups around the world. Within a few days the assembled company departed to wherever was home! But there was to be one other extraordinary incident. This concerned the beak of the Dove, the symbol that Sharon (who had never previously been to England), had seen for the conference many weeks before, while she was still in Vancouver.

Some six weeks after the Raven's Ait conference ended, I was shown a rather obscure document illustrating something that I had previously not been aware of. It was a book describing the Kingston Zodiac, a huge circle of arcane symbols over five miles in diameter, spread across the geography of West London. Many of the symbols are not those normally associated with astrology; they are more like the shamanic concept of 'power animals'.

One of these symbols was in the town of Kingston itself, near the river – a huge dove, laid out in the topography, its origins lost in history. Raven's Ait, when seen from above, is positioned *just over the beak of the dove;* something nobody had known at the time of the conference, and the very phrase that Sharon had used time and again in communicating her vision! And *the symbolism of the Dove and the Raven together – representing light and dark energies –* was just too powerful and poignant for words, in the context of what we had all experienced at that gathering!

As I have stated earlier, my feeling about this being Asphondel is that he is of great power and integrity, and willing to co-create. It seems to be his specific task, as a leader from the dark angelic side, to represent them in our joint activity of bringing an end to the phenomenon of separation.

ASPHONDEL AND THE CHILD

Around September of 1995, I visited my colleague Neris. When I looked at her son, I immediately recognised the energy of Asphondel – by a process of experiencing familiar energetic feelings, which I then was able to track back to where I had felt them previously – and told her what I saw.

She said that the energy being whose energy I had sensed as being present in her son had visited her house, appearing before her a number of times. The being appeared to her as a Black Knight with a bright silver sword. He had never communicated in any clear way up to this point.

As we continued our conversation, she looked startled, and then, after a few silent but very meaningful moments, said that the being was now present, and wished to talk with me. Let me say here I have absolutely no doubts about Neris, and we were sitting in an area where there is a known energy vortex which has been fully protected, and has been identified through the question/answer techniques of my dowsing as being a 'transdimensional gateway': meaning that beings from other dimensions can access us through it, if we are willing and sufficiently tuned in!

Neris agreed to channel the being so I could talk to him. He talked with great clarity and incisiveness. Included was information about Herculobus (see

Chapters 7 & 9) and the fourth-dimensional energies. We spoke in a very direct way – not like channelling in the normal sense that I have experienced it at all, more like direct telepathy – for about ten minutes.

The following day I talked to Neris again. She and her husband had a dream-filled night. This being, who now identified himself as Asphondel, was present several times. His messages were as follows:

"I am a messenger for what you call the dark, and for Lucifer. Lucifer is the equal and brother of Archangel Michael, and took on the divine task of causing separation, so that humanity could make its journey.

There can be no true unity on Earth while you continue to separate the light from the dark.

When you are trying to achieve unity, you are inviting humanity to join in with the divine will. This is part of the ascension of humanity.

You must learn to lose your fear. The key safe-guard is to co-create. In your invocations you should invoke unity in the name of the divine will, and you will be protected."

Neris was then shown the new chakra system, due to emerge as a result of the integrated energies resonating them into place in the human body: in effect, a complete energy restructuring of the human body was being predicted. In the morning there was a further great surprise. Neris found that her son had laid out all his toy building sticks and bricks in precisely the same pattern as the new chakra system shown by Asphondel, on his bedroom floor!

There is, I truly believe, something we might regard as 'real evil'; that 'manufactured' force I have spoken of, created by centuries of separation, the further polarisation of 'Light and Dark' to become 'Good and Evil' as part of the traumatic progress being played out by humanity. This has caused us to manifest these dark energies that are an aberration, that have intelligence, and are quite separate from the 'dark angels'. We are responsible for their existence! It is our fear that feeds them, and allows them to be; but this was always a part of the plan, and not, I suggest, a matter for guilt. I believe that the power of this aberrational force is now leaking rapidly away, as humanity shifts its consciousness to a higher, more positive level, but it will still take time to leave us completely.

As the forces of separation recede, there will be various attempts to bring them back into ascendancy, which I believe are doomed to fail. However, situations such as the recent warring in Bosnia is a demonstration of this. The area has been laced with this energy. The reassuring thing is that although these war zones are as nasty as any we have seen (and far more public because of the international nature of television), they are progressively getting far smaller. And because we are now witnessing what is happening through our televisions, our consciousness is being developed so that we will no longer provide the energetic support on which such wars thrive.

Quazar had something to tell us about dealing with the Luciferic Hierarchy, in an interesting conversation on 16th September 1995:

Peter: *Quazar, we have been having a lot of communication through the being Asphondel, and another being known as Perseus, that purport to come from the Luciferic hierarchy. I would like to discuss these communications with you. I would like to cross check them, and get your perspective, because, not only are we communicating with them, but we are now being asked to participate in certain actions. Can you first tell us if these communications are real, and in integrity?*

Quazar: *Well, we ask you to look at what you mean by the word 'integrity'.*

Peter: *Then, perhaps that's an incorrect word. Shall we say 'being made in good faith' by these beings?*

Quazar: *These beings will always make their suggestions in good faith; just as we make our suggestions in good faith. You now understand when you are dealing with high beings, whichever side of the light-dark dynamic they claim to come from. You have learned that those of a high order will never make suggestions of a formal kind, and you have learned what are proper and right interactions, in line with universal consciousness and laws. These you understand, and we expect you to apply the same impeccable standards to communications with all beings of the integrated Christ light.*

   You have no excuses if you allow yourselves to be misled. No-one will give you answers, and no-one will tell you what to do, unless they do so in a way that is not part of the universal laws, and is not to be followed. You know the importance of your own 'discernment' as you call it. You are now being tested, Peter, in ways that will stretch you, and build on all your experiences to date.

Peter: *Good! Well, Quazar, my discernment, to date, is that although what we are being told may stretch us in terms of its credibility, it is now something we are quite good at dealing with, I think..*

The point being made is that we can start to deal with these beings, if we work with care and integrity on both sides. The experience from Raven's Ait had shown us that the Luciferic angels, too, wished to start the process of integration. Indeed, we can only move forward with them, otherwise we cannot put an end to separation. In essence, their job is now over; the direct brief from God, to create separation so that the human experiment could proceed, is complete. The hierarchy that we have consigned to be held in darkness: they, too, want to 'come home' – and in the context of integration, it is essential that they do so!

So here we are, tasked with 'cleaning up' our act, based on the need for integrating the dark and the light. Quazar has the last say, from a communication on June 4th, 1995:

Quazar: *With all cleansing, the clean energy needs to come in to wash away that, we don't wish to call it dirty, we mean the other energy. Clean energy is an energy which is integrated light and dark together, not just the light alone...well, this is of complexity because of your misuse of the language to mean so many different things.*

The Christ light, we may (re)define now as the combination of the twelve energies that are the primary archetypes of the universe, both in their positive, if you will, and negative manifestations, an integration of dark and light. This is what we call the clean energy, that washes through the old 'light' and 'dark' which have been separate. When the light is separate from the dark, you do not actually have the Christ energy present.

If you will recall the work of the being Christ who walked the earth, he embraced the dark at all times. He acknowledged his own darkness. He forsook his life in his place on the cross, in asking and doubting God's love of him, and believing he had been forsaken by God. He demonstrated the integration of the presence of the dark with the light; one and the same working integratedly together, as the Christ energy. And so it is, that when you ask 'what can you do', it starts with each human being, in consciousness, embracing both their dark and light, and being always present with both, neither denying the love, or denying their fear. Only when the two are integrated, in one human being after another, will the integration occur everywhere. And through this, through your integration, and through your movement over the planet, physically going from one place to another as an integrating being (because it is not a finite process), you will be integrating, and as you integrate, you will discover more dark (as you call it), and you will discover more light, and then you will move and integrate the two, and so you move on.

As you physically walk the earth, taking with you this integration experience from one place to another – like carrying water and washing it through the hair to cleanse it of its dirt – so the human being who is integrating can move over the planet with his or her aura, which is so vast, and as you are integrating gets vaster and vaster. So as you walk the planet all who come within your aura, which may be (many) tens of feet around you, those people will themselves start cleansing, integrating, because you are like fresh water going through them.

Peter: *Quazar, the teacher Arnold Patent spoke to us about the ability to transmute energies into a positive form, and the need to be in the places where the biggest energies were running in order to have the greatest transformational effect. I think that what you have just said mirrors that, and relates it to Sarajevo. Is that correct?*

Quazar: *It is, but your role is not to transform dark into the light. This is a form of denial, trying to shift everything from dark to light. The time of dark/ light, male/female, yin/yang is now over in the sense of separation. It is the time of integrating these energies into one. Neither is wrong: the dark has had to be present, it is a necessary condition for the light to be present. It is not bad or evil, in the way in which you separate it. It is part of you and it is time to integrate it as such.*

Peter: *Thank you, Quazar, that's a very important distinction, and one that we had not really focused on. This integration of light and dark: has this phenomena which is now beginning to happen on this planet happened many times elsewhere, or is this genuinely something new?*

Quazar: *It is for the consciousness of the humanoid, the earth, because humans of all forms on this planet have been allowed to experience, uniquely, this power of the dark, with free will.*

Peter: *So the uniqueness is the involvement of free will in this process...It seems to us that many in other realms who have viewed this free will experiment have perhaps had great reservations about it?*

Quazar: *Indeed.*

Peter: *Is it correct that this experiment has been tried in other places, and has never succeeded?*

Quazar: *It has not been so, in the way that we have participated in this place.*

Peter: *The whole human experiment here is unique?*

Quazar: *Indeed.*

Peter: *In recent years we have heard many predictions of a dramatic end to this planet. Are we now past the point where the 'Armageddon' view of what happens next is an option?*

Quazar: *Indeed, you are moving away from the total annihilation of the human species on this planet.*

Peter: This is the sense that we have had as well, so thank you for confirming it.

It seems that a great deal is going on at the magical, and energy levels, and this is rapidly being translated into great and accelerating change in our physical plane of existence. Better yet, the much predicted great apocalyptic ending has almost certainly been avoided. We, humanity, have turned the corner, have ended the long and often agonising phenomenon of 'The Fall'. We now have the task of reversing our own experience of separation, and we have this new Christ energy anchored on the planet to support and assist us in this task!

So I suggest we all try to see what is happening to all of us as being like the final graduation. We have been through all the forms and grades of this great school called planet Earth, in many, many incarnations. We have all had the experience of journeying through those many lives, and the changing energies around us are beginning to allow us to access all of that experience, and much more besides. We have everything we need to make it: only a few short steps left to graduation day! And I truly believe that this heralds a stunning transformation, with humanity moving to its next level, and becoming very different from what we are now.

It seems to me that the only way from here is up!

FORWARDS!

Remind us of what you, too,

forgot you know

So that you can let go

forget,

the way things were.

For you to now flow,

on from there...

...And grow into

life's joy,

we are all meant to share!

Epilogue – On The Transformation Of Humanity

All the information in this book speaks, indirectly and sometimes directly, of the transformation of humanity into a form potentially very different from that with which we are familiar, a challenging concept for many. This document first came to us through the *Internet*, although in the original it was somewhat longer. I don't actually know where on the planet this information was first delivered, but it seems to me to be deeply wise and loving, the criteria that I always recommend for high quality channelling. I think it offers a really solid perspective about all that is happening, and how to handle it. I have no hesitation in reproducing some of it here, with grateful thanks to the original authors for making it public, and as a suitable summary of the core message of this book:

Guidance from the Golden Star Alliance

The Golden Star Alliance is an aspect of the Council of the Stellar Ring. This is a vast intergalactic council whose members are both extraterrestrial and angelic in origin, and it also includes an Ascended Master who originally sources from planet Earth. Most of the beings on this council had dense, third-dimensional bodies at one time, which, through the process of Ascension, they transformed into their present state, which is as immortal bodies of Light. Now, those beings have gathered together to support the evolution of planets.

We have come here at this time to support beings in the ecstatic transformation that is taking place on planet Earth. Many of you also chose to come here to assist with this process. Now is the time to release the armour of dysfunctionality that you have been wearing, and to step forward into the Light of your Magnificence.

We would like to tell you a story. It may help you to remember...

THE COSMIC DAY

Once upon a time we were all part of one magnificent glowing orb of golden light. And ALL THAT IS, in its desire for even more knowingness of itself decided to try an experiment. One day this vast brilliance shot millions and millions of tiny pieces of itself, like dazzling shooting stars, in all directions throughout the universe, creating a light show like none other. Each of these aspects of the One went on an incredible journey through solar systems and beyond, travelling farther and farther from Source, and then returning to be reunited in a magnificent celebration of Light. From this experiment, the consciousness of ALL THAT IS expanded in many ways, and therefore it was able to view The Whole from other, new perspectives – and hence come to know itself more fully.

At the start of the journey, each spark of Light had full remembrance of ALL THAT IS. However, as sparks journeyed farther and farther from the Source they took on more form, more density, becoming more physical. They began to forget they were a part of the One. On and on they spun through time and space, ever condensing, ever materialising, until finally they reached a point of maximum separation. Everything that took them to that point was a part of what they had become as unique crystalisations of energy. If this entire journey from the Source and back took one day on the cosmic clock, this moment would be 'high noon'. From this point on, each individualised aspect of ALL THAT IS begins its journey home, with ever-increasing recognition and knowingness of the Light. Earth is one such unit in consciousness. For aeons it has been condensing into matter. But twelve noon of the cosmic day has just past. More good news: we are going home!

There was much support for the planet in reaching its point of maximum separation, and so too is there much support in bringing her home.

PLANET EARTH: DISTORTIONAL LIMITATION SYSTEM 101

As the planet condensed, beings had the option of coming here to experience limitation; a system based on the denial of their own Magnificence. Then, as the veils were lifted, they would experience more knowingness, more love and recognition of ALL THAT IS than ever before and their journey home could be filled with joy.

A tremendous amount is required of beings who choose this path. You need to forget that you are one with the Source, and that you decided to come here. You leave behind an existence based on love and come to a place that allows fear, pain and suffering, judgement and denial, separation, abandonment, death and destruction. Nothing could prepare you for this devastation. At the core of your beingness, you felt abandoned by ALL THAT IS as you experienced the pain of separation. And from that place you built a reality based on fear for your very survival. BUT YOU WERE NOT ALONE.

And now, as the Earth is moving into its homeward voyage, there is the opportunity to shed these limitations and to master expression of your own Divine Spirit.

PLANETARY TRANSITIONING

On a planetary scale, a massive shift is taking place as the veils of separation and denial are lifting.

First you had to forget who you were, or why you were here. Then you had to engage with a totally distortional system and identify yourself to be a struggling human. Now you must wake up and begin the process of transmuting these distortions and patterns that are no longer functional or desired in the co-creation of a new world! And remember: you volunteered for the job. If you hadn't had complete faith in your own strength and courage, you wouldn't be here now.

THE WAKE-UP CALL

As the earth passes twelve noon on the Cosmic Clock and is returning home to the Source, so too all life forms on this planet are in various stages of radical transformation. There is a transmutation taking place in the very cells of your body. Information that was coded in the DNA of your structure is now being activated. That is why so many of you are now waking up and remembering.

TRANSMUTATION OF DENSE PHYSICAL BODIES INTO LIGHT

These are very exciting times and incredible changes are taking place. Most of you have been experiencing them on one level or another. We would like to discuss some of these changes so you may have more understanding of them. Remember, your own experiences are determined by your particular function and design, so they may not look anything like what we describe here. We do not wish to alarm you with all this talk of transmutation, but instead would like to gently prepare you for what is occurring; precisely because these changes ARE occurring. Even scientists admit that "something" is going on. They are discovering new proteins and amino-acids in the body, for example, that they think they must have overlooked before. However, they are NEW proteins and amino acids, for you are being chemically re-structured and enhanced!

THE QUICKENING

You humans are high-energy transformers, like sponges in the energy sea around you. As more and more light, the incoming new energy, becomes available to you, the more the intensity of the electromagnetic energy around you also increases. Any changes in the surrounding energetic field are picked up by the subtle or etheric body, which acts as a receiver, assimilator and transmitter of these energies.

These changes directly affect the physical body, which is the outward manifestation of the etheric level. Due to the increased energies present, the etheric body is vibrating at a higher frequency, and the physical body is trying to catch up but hasn't quite done so yet. This results in a speeding up of your molecular structure.

CHAKRAS AS TRANSMITTERS AND RECEIVERS

As we have mentioned, the etheric body acts as a transmitter and receiver for the energies. This takes place via specific energy centres or chakras. Each chakra is directly associated with an endocrine gland and a nerve plexus. Because of their close relationship with the chakras, which transmit and receive this energy, the endocrine and nervous systems are also undergoing radical transmutation. The increase in electrical energies requires a complete re-wiring of the nervous system. It is important to acknowledge the changes and to support the physical body as much as possible.

RESTRUCTURING THE ENDOCRINE SYSTEM

Certain energy centres will be affected more than others at different times as the shifts take place. For example, the base, or first chakra is in many of you being radically transformed at this present time. It manifests externally in the physical body as the adrenal glands, which are related to security and survival and your ability to deal with stress.

As they transmute, there may be periods when you feel more anxious and irritable than usual; restless, headachy, less able to concentrate; have an increased sensitivity to people, sounds, smells and environment; experience joint pains, muscle soreness (particularly low back), or poor digestion. During these times the body may require certain nutrients – fats, proteins, carbohydrates, vitamins, minerals and hormones – that it didn't need before. So you may experience intense cravings for certain foods, some of which you may not normally eat!

The fifth, or throat chakra is also a very powerful centre, and its physical counterpart, the thyroid gland, is particularly vulnerable to changes in electromagnetic energy. This gland regulates the metabolic processes of the body, and some of the transmutative symptoms that commonly result are unexplained weight gain or loss, sluggishness, altered sleep patterns, and again, feelings of increased tiredness and fatigue.

These are examples of a few things you may experience as a new blueprint is laid down for the physical body. Honour the changes that are taking place. Read a good book or watch a movie. And know that this too, will pass.

NEW PATHWAYS: REWIRING THE NERVOUS SYSTEM

The body picks up the energies moving in, around and through it via sensory nerves which carry impulses from the peripheral systems of the body into the grey matter of the Central Nervous System.

As more and more light is available, the intensity of electromagnetic energy around you increases. This means more rapid neurological activity in the body resulting in higher intensity impulses firing into the Central Nervous System, which will immediately attempt to dissipate that energy by sending it back out of the spinal chord.

If these impulses then fire along facilitated pathways into the muscular system, they could cause muscle tightness and soreness. If they fire into the blood vessels, restricted circulation can results. When these impulses fire into the skin, you may feel unusually hot or cold, pricking, itching etc. And if they fire into the organs and glands, they may inhibit their previously normal functioning in some of the ways we have already discussed.

SEEING BEYOND THE VEILS

These increased energies affect all aspects of your being in this transmutation. With higher vibrational frequencies comes increased awareness on all levels. Many of you still rely on old perceptual references, however, as your multidimensional awareness increases and the veils lift, you will have more experiences of seeing beyond them. You may have moments of "slipping out of time and space". Some of you have experienced this already. At times it seems like hours have gone by, but only a few minutes of linear time have passed. The opposite happens when time just disappears and you don't know where it went. You may feel like you have been caught in a time warp.

EMBRACE YOUR WHOLENESS

As each spark of Light left Source and condensed deeper and deeper into matter and limitation, it made certain choices and decisions based on what was happening around it. As all the sparks did this, the configuration of energies that made up each individual unit of consciousness was totally unique. Like a snowflake that falls from the sky, none was like any other, and each had its own perfect Divine Design.

You are one of those sparks of consciousness. While experiencing limitation, many of you interpreted your uniqueness as things that were wrong with you and set about trying to 'fix' them. However, you discovered they are part of your core structure. You try to manipulate and control these aspects of self, but they never really change. They are what's right and absolutely perfect about you, and they may become your greatest assets and strengths in the new world.

By honouring your Divine Design, you honour your Wholeness. By honouring your Wholeness, you recognise the Oneness of all life.

TRANSMUTING PATHWAYS IN CONSCIOUSNESS

Each of you in your uniqueness is more attuned to certain energies than others. Like having an antenna calibrated to receive a particular station, many of you resonate with different wavelengths and different vibrational frequencies. Whatever wavelengths your particular design is calibrated to are pathways cut in consciousness. Once you begin to transmute the energies of those particular frequencies, the universe will take advantage of these pathways to transmute more and more of the same energies. So it may appear that issues you thought you had dealt with and resolved have suddenly re-emerged bigger than life, with even more intensity and drama than before. Recognise that energies are present and let them move through you.

Occasionally you may experience waves of grief or sadness. Things you once valued that are no longer supportive will leave your energy field. Whole aspects of your life that no longer work for you are falling away.

Remember: consciousness is energy, emotions are energy, thoughts and feelings are energy. As you integrate the higher frequencies, all aspects of self will undergo major shifts and changes. Honour the magnitude of what is taking place.

PATTERN BREAKING

Your mental, physical and emotional bodies are wonderful barometers for Spirit, and each are vehicles through which ALL THAT IS expresses on this plane. In a limitation system where energies were condensing and many veils were in place, much of this valuable data from Spirit was denied, especially from the emotional body.

When an emotional experience is repressed, its vibratory rate becomes slower and slower until it goes below conscious level and forms a dark energetic crystal, with the entire experience compressed and stored in the nervous system, soft tissues, organs and glands of the body. There it lies dormant, waiting to be reactivated later.

There are a number of ways in which these dark crystals are triggered; the tone of someone's voice, the way a person looks or acts, a smell, a thought, a touch, a feeling. Once triggered, the vibratory rate of the crystallised energy speeds up and is brought back to consciousness. At that point, although things appear very real to you, you are actually caught up in a re-run, and are reacting to karmically repressed energies that are contained in the cells of your body.

Now, as the quickening takes place and your body begins to vibrate at more refined frequencies, these repressed, denied aspects also quicken and become amplified. They need to vibrate out. Touch, colour, light, breath and movement can be used as doorways through which these energies can be accessed to release these dark energetic crystals into light and to restructure patterns of consciousness that will support your highest expression.

As more of you awaken to your Divine Mission and Purpose here, we suspect that many new and powerful technologies will be brought forth. And remember, if all the dense, crystallised energies held in your body were released into the Light, you would have – a Light Body!

MORE TRANSMUTIVE SYMPTOMS

As shifts take place and your body vibrates at another frequency, there may be times when it feels denser and heavier than usual, although no noticeable physical changes have taken place. Or you may feel suddenly lighter as energies are released and shed. At times it may even feel like you have stepped into someone else's body!

Mood swings are also symptomatic of the body's attempts to integrate more light. Other reactions to the increased intensity are flu-like symptoms, sinusitis and congestion, aches and pains, and feelings of toxicity. The body is reaching a threshold. It will pass beyond this as its capacity to handle more light increases. At these times especially it is useful to drink lots of water. There is a sloughing off taking place on a cellular level. Water helps to facilitate this, both drinking and bathing. Take more baths. Go swimming. Water is wonderful to balance your energy, to soothe and relax.

Ringing or tones in the ears are often transmissions from other dimensions. This information often makes itself known to you at the appropriate time.

You might be in the middle of a sentence when...you completely forget what you were going to say next. Or you may be thinking about something that happened when...you have difficulty accessing the memory to it. As we move into a state of grace, the harder it is to reference the past. All useless data is gradually being taken from the files. You may find that much of your remaining memory is going 'off line', and it takes concentration to retrieve it.

You may be fully absorbed in something, when...the energy is gone, your interest dies. This could be a message from Spirit that there is no longer alignment with what you are doing, and it is not the highest possibility for where your energies could be. So Spirit simply pulls the plug.

A NEW CONTEXT FOR HEALING

We mention these symptoms because many of you are experiencing them as something that is wrong with you and that needs to be 'fixed', and are looking for someone or something to heal you. We don't think you need to be healed because we don't think there is anything wrong with you. All is in alignment with the Divine Plan. If you identify with what you think is wrong with you, you may find yourself going down with the part that is dying.

However, discernment is required. If you do think you need medical assistance, there are many in the healing professions (bodyworkers, acupuncturists, homeopaths, and naturopaths, for example) who are conscious of these shifts and may be of support to you.

DISCERNMENT

Speaking of discernment, we would point out that many of these symptoms of evolution could also be symptoms of you not following your own Spirit. Or they may indicate that undermining energies are present. Trust your own knowing. Doubt is the chief of the undermining energies, and is not a natural state to be in. Follow whatever you think is your Spirit until you know otherwise.

SUPPORTING YOUR BODY DURING SHIFTS

Your body's needs will probably change rapidly during these times. We have already mentioned that you may have weird cravings for foods you don't normally eat. You may have a huge appetite one day and hardly be hungry the next. You might find yourself sleeping many more hours than usual and having to take naps during the day, and then needing very little sleep at all and having an abundance of energy. It is most important to stay in touch moment to moment. Your body will guide you to the foods and support it needs. Listen to it.

We have mentioned the importance of drinking lots of water. Physical exercise is also supportive, be it walking, jogging, running, hiking, swimming, or dancing. The latter is particularly powerful because through dance many new energetic pathways are cut and integrated in the body.

DIVINE TIMING

As the planet starts to journey back to the Source, everyone who chooses to stay here and remain in a body will also go through these shifts. However, each person has his/her own 'high noon'. Some beings passed noon many centuries ago; others will not reach it for many years to come. It is important to honour the Divine Timing of these shifts and changes. You may find that some patterns are not ready to be released yet. Honour your Wholeness. Recognise that it is all part of the Divine Plan unfolding.

THE STARSEEDS FOR A NEW CIVILIZATION

As you grow more and more into following your Spirit without hesitation, doing everything in each moment because you were Divinely guided to do so as opposed to following your ego/personality's wishes, you will find your life to be more ecstatic, more joyous, more emotional, more passionate, more intense, more dramatic than ever before. Transpersonal does not mean boring! You are the starseeds for a new civilisation!

THE BIRTH OF A NEW ERA

You are in the midst of great changes – the most radical period of change in your planet's history. The old world is dying. It will happen: let it do so gracefully. As more and more energies from other dimensions enter into this plane, much of what you have known and held on to will fall away giving birth to a new, higher octave of expression.

Many will cling to and try to 'save' the old world that is dying, for though it is filled with illusions of duality and separation, it is familiar, and to step into the new world often means leaping into the Unknown.

One of the keys in making this transition is to recognise your fascinations; to everything you consciously and unconsciously accept as reality. What do you make real in your life? What do you focus your energies on?

Consider that what you previously thought of as real is no more than an audio-visual hologram of consciousness; a *picture* of reality. You think in pictures, and form your inner reality from these pictures. All you do, how you think, feel, and act, and what you manifest in the world around you, is affected by the pictures you hold as true.

All those images that you agreed with as being 'real' have become stored in the conscious and unconscious mind and form the basis for your current reality. Many of you don't see them as optional images, or pictures of reality, but consider them 'real'. However, they are optional. You can change them.

To fully engage in the new world requires that you be conscious of the images that you put your attention on. All That Is, in its desire to love and support you, wants you to have it all, and presumes that your attention is on what you want. It will therefore rearrange itself to manifest even more of the same. Whatever you lend your fascination to, whatever you label or define as reality, you'll get more of. If you focus your energies on that which is dying, you only prolong the inevitable.

THE GATHERING OF MASTERS

The time we have been waiting for is upon us. There is a Great Gathering taking place. Planet Earth has become a focal point throughout this universe and beyond. Due to the incredible diversity of species here, many beings from other planets and dimensions are offering their support and assistance at this time.

A great number of beings presently incarnated on this plane are aspects of and representatives or focal points for whole councils of entities on the other dimensions. It is time to wake up to the vast multidimensional master that you are. Yes, you are human, but you are also so much more. You came here with a Divine Mission. Part of that was to go unconscious and forget who you were and why you were here. Now is the time to remember. Stand up and step forward into the Light of your Magnificence. Embody all that you truly are. The time that you have been preparing for is NOW.

YOUR SEED VISION LEADS YOU HOME

All that is required of you is that you take that initial leap, that leap into the Unknown. Sooner or later you will all face that choice. And if you are lucky, there will be no choice. For a voice is calling you. It is Your Voice. It tells you to look within. And there, in each of you, is a Seed Vision which speaks of something you have longed for, ached for, burned for. Something that has always carried you forth when it appeared as if all the odds were stacked against you. Something that has called out to that precious part deep within you, giving you faith, courage and strength to go on. That piece...is the Spark of Light...which will lead you Home.

We love you...and we welcome you Home.

The Golden Star Alliance.

THE END

An Invitation

Through the process of telling the stories in this book, and others, to various groups of people, I have learned how nearly everyone has had some unusual experience; whether it be a ghostly encounter, a telepathic communication, remarkable sequences of coincidences, or some kind of out-of-body experience. This phenomenon is widespread, endemic to the task of being human.

Yet in our 'modern' society we do not talk about these experiences, indeed, many of these people are regarded as being mad. It is most disturbing to hear voices, and not to have any support in dealing with the phenomenon. For many of these people I believe something else is taking place, something which is essentially not illness-related, and can be controlled with the right support and handling.

It seems to me to be essential that we all start talking about the strange things we experience. The world is changing, and strange happenings are becoming even more commonplace. We need to get things out in the open, come clean, and make it all right for people to talk about what has happened to them.

So, here is one thing you can do to help. If you have had a strange experience, and are willing to have it published, write to us at the address in the front of this book, and tell us about it. We may be able to use your story in future books in the 'Adventures' series. And encourage people to talk about these things freely.

Peter R-D